ADVANCE PRAISE

"Gritty, raw and authentically emotional, this book will shatter your heart and then leave it open, softened, and hopeful. It is an honest portrayal of mental illness and its ripple effects through a family, and a testament to a daughter's brave decision to break old patterns, seek help, and trust her higher power in the wake of her father's death."

—Michelle M. Olsen, CPCC, MA,
Career & Life Coach

"*Trusting Resilience* is a powerful story of a daughter›s love and determination in finding support and treatment for her mother battling schizophrenia. Navigating mountains of paperwork, jumping through legal hoops and waiting for hours on hold, Ms. Moore exemplifies fierce grit and gentle forgiveness reminding us that though imperfect, family is worth fighting for!"

—Stacey Burdette, LLPC,
Stacey Burdette Counseling

"In this moving story about mental health and its impact on family, Heather and Susan embark on a journey of courage, trust, resilience, strength, pain, healing, surrender, discovery, transformation, and love. Inspiring and heartbreaking at times, I felt moved by the author's internal struggles and the very heavy burden of ancestral and family karma she carried, as she desperately tried to help her undiagnosed mentally ill mother, navigating many obstacles with minimal support, through a failed and cruel system that needs to change. It's a story of forgiveness and miracles, and I highly recommend this book."

—Soreliz Ascanio, LCSW, MA,
Children's Hospital Oakland, California

TRUSTING RESILIENCE

TRUSTING RESILIENCE

Schizophrenia, Family, and
the Journey to Love

HEATHER MOORE

Trusting Resilience: Schizophrenia, Family, and the Journey to Love
Published by Luminosity Press
Grand Rapids, Michigan, U.S.A.

MOORE, HEATHER, Author
TRUSTING RESILIENCE
HEATHER MOORE

Library of Congress Control Number: 2025923711

ISBN: 979-8-9938083-0-7, 979-8-9938083-2-1 (paperback)
ISBN: 979-8-9938083-3-8 (hardcover)
ISBN: 979-8-9938083-1-4, 979-8-9938083-4-5 (digital)

PSYCHOLOGY / Psychopathology / Schizophrenia
FAMILY & RELATIONSHIPS / Dysfunctional Families
BODY, MIND & SPIRIT / Inspiration & Personal Growth
HEALTH & FITNESS / Mental Health

Editing: Susan Crossman (crossmancommunications.com)
Cover Design: Julia Kuris (designerbility.com.au)
Interior & E-book formatting: Amit Dey (amitdey2528@gmail.com)
Project Management/Consulting: Susie Schaefer (finishthebookpublishing.com)

QUANTITY PURCHASES: Schools, companies, professional groups, clubs, and other organizations may qualify for special terms when ordering quantities of this title. For information, email info@luminositypress.com

DEDICATION

This book is dedicated to all of the children who are born to a parent with mental illness. Their illness is not your fault. There is nothing wrong with you, you are not broken, bad, or ugly.

You are not alone.

You are holy, worthy and deserving.

You are loved.

CONTENTS

Mom

Appendix

TRUSTING RESILIENCE

trust·ing /ˈtrəstiNG/
adjective

showing or tending to have a belief in a person's honesty or sincerity; not suspicious.

"it is foolish to be too trusting of other people"

re·sil·ience /rəˈzilēən(t)s/
noun

1. the capacity to withstand or to recover quickly from difficulties; toughness.
   "the remarkable resilience of so many institutions"

2. the ability of a substance or object to spring back into shape; elasticity.
   "nylon is excellent in wearability and resilience"

Trusting resilience means believing in your own ability to recover from adversity while trusting the support of others and the systems you are part of. This involves self-trust in your capacity to cope, as well as trusting reliable relationships and communities to provide support during challenging times.

It is the inner fortitude that allows you to adapt and over-come difficulties, built on both personal strength and the strength of your connections. Building this trust allows for a more confident, less fearful approach to adversity, where resiliency is a natural human state, not a trait to be developed.

DISCLAIMER

This book details the author's personal opinions, and she makes no representations or warranties of any kind with respect to this book or its contents. The statements made in this book are not intended to diagnose, treat, cure, or prevent any physical, mental, emotional, or spiritual condition or unhappiness. They are meant to share one family's story and do not replace medical care or therapy.

All content is for informational and educational purposes and does not establish any kind of patient/client relationship. The information presented here is not a substitute for any kind of professional advice. Please consult with your own therapist or other healthcare specialist regarding the suggestions and experiences shared in this book. Before you begin any program, or change your lifestyle in any way, you should consult your physician or another licensed practitioner to ensure you are in good health and that the information contained in this book will not harm you.

Except as specifically stated in this book, neither the author, the editor, nor the publisher, nor any authors, contributors, or other representatives, will be liable for damages arising out of or in connection with the use of this book.

This is a comprehensive limitation of liability that applies to all damages of any kind, including (without limitation) compensatory; direct, indirect, or consequential damages; loss of data, income, or profit; loss of or damage to property, and claims of third parties.

If you are experiencing severe anxiety and depression or an immediate crisis, please reach out to a mental health professional, a crisis center, or a hotline.

Although this book brings forward a story that can at times be heartbreaking, and it discusses a topic than can make many people uncomfortable, please be assured that there is grace and goodness woven through every page and that the ending leaves the reader with a positive understanding of the majesty of our world, as well as a positive sense of closure and a generous serving of hope for the future.

CHAPTER 1

THE LAST TIME

May 24, 2015

I picked up my phone and punched in the numbers to my parents' place back in Michigan. My father would probably be sitting in his favorite chair, reading the newspaper or watching TV, and my mother would likely be busy in the kitchen. I had another call to get to and speaking with my parents was not something I raced to do. But something told me it was time to check in, and years of meditative practice had taught me to trust my gut.

"Hey, Dad."

"Hey, Heather, how are you?"

"I'm good."

"What're you up to?" We had only exchanged a few words but already I could tell something wasn't right. My dad's voice over the phone sounded strained and although I was glad I had called, I felt my internal world shift.

"I've just been busy with work. And hanging out with friends. You still have that nasty cough. It sounds like pneumonia. I'm getting worried." Worried didn't come close to covering what I was feeling. Dad had been diagnosed with an aggressive cancer of the ureter a dozen years earlier and had already undergone numerous operations. Doctors had removed the offending ureter, as well as one kidney and his bladder; although he was still pretty functional, I'd noticed he was getting sick a lot, and he admitted to being tired all the time.

"Have you gone to the doctor yet?" I asked.

"No, not yet. I've got an appointment for next Tuesday," he said. "Can't seem to get my energy up these days, although I went to the party Kelly and Dan had yesterday afternoon. We chit chatted and had some food and a beer. It was really fun."

Kelly was my cousin and Dan was her partner. I liked them a lot—in fact I liked pretty much all my dad's family—but living in California meant I hardly ever got to see them.

"I'm glad you're having a good time, Dad. You deserve it."

"Are you dating anyone yet?" he asked, subtly changing the topic of conversation. "I worry about you, being alone out West. I know I raised you to be independent, but don't you want to spend your life with someone?"

"Of course! I'd love to find someone and get married, and I feel like I'm ready now." For years I'd told myself finding a healthy mature man in the Bay area was damn near impossible. But the truth was, I was deeply terrified of being trapped in a loveless lifelong commitment. My parents' marriage had not been a great example of what happens after people say, "I do." What made finding someone even more challenging was my lengthy list of criteria. A few years before I had dated a man who I considered a masculine God, and I had felt my femininity in surprising ways, although he hadn't been an ideal match. To be with someone who actually knew how to hold me energetically in a way that allowed my sensuality to express naturally and effortlessly made it hard to go back to "the average." He showed me a part of myself that was delicious and powerful. I'd been hooked.

"I want a man's man," I joked.

Dad laughed. "You want someone like me?"

Umm, not exactly. But I chuckled at his sweetness. "Yes, Dad, I want someone just like you."

"Well, I hope you find him. Do you want to talk to Mom?"

"No, I'll talk to her later. I have to go. I love you so much, Dad. Sleep well."

"I love you too, talk later."

This was the last conversation I had with my father. I got off the phone and burst into tears. My whole being shattered. Dad was dying, I didn't know how I knew it, but I did. It was imminent. I asked myself if there was anything I hadn't told him, anything that needed to be set right in our relationship. I felt a delicate inner, "no." But I was devastated and there was an indescribable pain in my chest. My dad had been a source of anger and misery in my life, and he had abdicated his responsibilities in countless ways along my path to adulthood. We had been able to find a path to love anyway.

I was due on my women's prayer circle call, a source of strength and support at the best of times so now, full of angst, and sobbing, I logged onto it. "My dad is going to die soon," I managed to choke out. "Please pray with me."

CHAPTER 2

RECONCILIATION

July 13, 2014

About a year earlier, I had gone to visit my parents in Michigan for a week in the summer. It had been a while since I'd been back, and I had been craving the hot summer nights I remembered from my childhood. They had always been filled with the blur of dancing fireflies, lighting my imagination with magic. I'd been in California almost twenty years by that point and as time went by I had visited Michigan less and less often. I loved my parents but, typically, after three or four days filled with conflict and disagreement, I would end up crying in a messy heap on the floor. Dad's judgment had a way of making me feel like a piece of shit, and Mom's illness made me feel like I was crazy.

This visit had been different. Before I left to go East, I had prayed to God to set our relationship right. I had prayed for us to connect in our hearts and open the historically closed doors between us so we could begin to know each other as adults. As equals. The sad truth was they had no idea who I was, and I knew only bits and pieces of what their lives had been like before I—their only child—had been born. I never saw them as separate, individual human beings, only as the characters of Mom-and-Dad, fulfilling their roles. It seems like a very childish and selfish viewpoint to me now. I didn't know their passions, what made them deeply happy, or how they felt about their lives in general. It brought up tremendous sadness in me, like a missed opportunity to get to know a part of who I was and where I had come from. My childhood had been traumatic. But I had matured and evolved, and I was sure they had, too. I longed to have a deep connected relationship with them.

One afternoon during my visit I put an exercise DVD in the player. Like most of Dad's things, the machine was old and didn't work very well. It mangled the disc, which then got stuck in the player. As I struggled to correct the problem, I could see Mom's reflection in the TV screen. She was sitting at the kitchen table, watching me. Over the years, all through my childhood, her typical response to seeing me in distress had been to do nothing. She had never had the emotional reactions of the archetypal mother who drops everything to help a crying child. Whenever a difficult situation would trigger tears of frustration and hurt, and I would run into my room, Dad would sail into view and ask Mom what had happened. He could never tolerate hearing me cry.

"I don't know," my mother would say defensively, as she did on this occasion. "Why don't you go ask her?" And so, Dad came into my room.

"What's wrong, Heather? What happened?" He looked so worried and gentle. His concern was beautiful and precious. I imagine it's how God feels for each one of us.

"The DVD player chewed up my exercise CD," I said through tears of frustration.

"Well, I'll buy you a new CD," he said. Instead of pushing him out the door, as I would have done at any point in the past, I saw an opportunity, and an answer to my prayers.

Trembling, I yelled, "It's not about the DVD!" I had trouble getting the words out. "It's about never feeling supported. You've watched me struggle for years and you aren't there for me."

"What do you want me to do?" he asked in anguish.

I paused, terrified. "I want you to hug me and tell me it's going to be okay," I said in surprise. No one had ever asked me what I wanted them to do and I hadn't expected this answer.

"Okay, I can do that," Dad said.

I stood up and walked over to my father and let him hold me. For the first time in my adult life, I let myself be vulnerable with him. My five-foot-four-inch frame standing over all five-foot-two-inches of him made me feel like a giant, but also like a little girl.

"It's all going to be okay," he said. "I love you. It's all going to be okay." He kept repeating it. I still can feel his tiny body, his skin, the touch of his hair against my face. We had never hugged like that before and I felt uncomfortable and awkward, but it was one of the most tender moments of my life, and it's been burned into my memory forever.

After I calmed down, I walked out into the living room. Dad followed.

"The three of us need to talk," I said. "If someone asked you if you know much about your daughter, what would you say?"

They hesitated, looking a little stunned. This was not a question someone was supposed to ask their parents, and they felt uncomfortable. And then both said, "No."

"Don't you think that's sad? I don't know you, either. I'm your only child and we are strangers. How are we going to change this?"

I spent the next few hours sharing with them what had happened over the previous twenty years of my life. Dad sat looking concerned as I recounted my miscarriage, the abortion, my battle with anorexia, the abusive relationships, and my addictions to drugs and alcohol. Mom looked oblivious, for the most part, but as she had always done when she didn't have a natural response of her own to something, she followed Dad's cues.

My parents are staunch Republican, NRA, Rush Limbaugh folk, so some of the things I shared with them blew their minds. I was especially apprehensive to share that I had had an abortion, knowing that Dad was very much against them.

"Don't you think abortions are murder?" he asked.

"I don't think of it that way," I said. "At the time I had no resources to raise a child, and I wasn't with someone I loved. Would you have wanted me to come home and live with you?" They both stared at me, like two deer caught in the headlights, mentally I could hear their thoughts: *hell no!*

Suddenly they both burst out laughing as they realized their own truth had been revealed. I smiled, relieved.

"Well, okay then! I made the right decision." I continued my story, explaining how I found Alcoholics Anonymous (AA) and got sober. I told them about the influential people in my life and why I love nature, what kinds of things interested me ... I told them anything I could think of that would allow me to stand completely naked and vulnerable in front of my parents and say, "this is me, this is the person you raised, and this is how she turned out."

"I wish you had told us," Dad said. "I would have liked to have been there for you." Mom nodded along.

The relief I felt in my being was indescribable: I felt heard and seen. I was sharing with them all my dirty little secrets and in return I felt love and devotion. Why had I waited this long?

In my twenties I had sent Dad two letters hoping to reconcile our relationship, but they were full of blame about all the ways he hadn't shown up for me the way I wanted him to. I never actually shared myself with him. I never let him *see me*, and this proved to be the key to healing our relationship.

My remaining days with my parents were blissful. We spent time talking outside in the garden. I helped Mom with the cooking and Dad with some shopping and yard work. It was fun being with Mom in the kitchen, which never had relinquished its 1970s harvest gold appliances and dark brown cabinets. Mom loved to teach me things about cooking, baking, and creating unusual dishes, and we laughed a lot in the process.

My parents had bought the house they were living in around 2005, my dad having lost my childhood home to bankruptcy in 1995. I had loved that house, and I still miss it terribly. When we had to leave, I felt like something in me died. It had been a small 1,000-square-foot ranch style home when they had bought it in 1977 and then when I was about four, they had remodeled and added another 2,000 square-feet with a huge deck out the back and a swimming pool. As a teenager, my house had been the party house, which both my parents seemed to like. That was one thing my parents had done well: they made my friends feel welcome. But, ultimately, a big house with a swimming pool doesn't make up for constant fights and paranoid accusations.

This trip brought an opportunity for healing. Maybe we could turn things around. My mother was a great cook and had even completed two years of a culinary arts program at one point, so when she was behaving relatively normally, we ate well. This trip saw us cooking together with comparatively few angry outbursts. Together we even devised a special tapas menu and prepared it together.

"This is fun, Momma. Have you ever made this stuff before?"

"No. It's what your father would refer to as 'different'." That was Dad's polite way of saying he didn't like something. He liked his food simple, like, beans-in-a-can simple. Serve him anything that had even a special sauce on it, and he'd say, "Oh. That's … different."

"You're so open-minded, Heather," Mom beamed. "When you're here I can be so much more creative in the kitchen."

I was planning on going to the Detroit Institute of Arts (DIA) for a photography exhibit I wanted to see and decided to invite Dad along. He accepted, to my surprise, and we happily got into his Ford Explorer and drove to Detroit. I remember the few times Dad and I had driven downtown together. We'd gone to a ballet at the Fox Theater my first Christmas home from San Diego, and we'd gone twice to Second City for a comedy show. We'd also gone to a Detroit Tigers baseball game when I had been eight years old. It had been raining and we were late. Dad was driving ninety miles an hour in our dark green 1975 Ford LTD Country Squire Station Wagon. He had been an amateur racecar driver before I was born, so I was used to it, but my friend, Laurie, who was going with us to the game, clung to the door for dear life.

On this visit, our trip to the DIA took place on a gorgeous summer day but driving down I-96 gave me a slightly haunted feeling. It's a ten-lane highway in some areas and there was no one on any of them. A friend calls it post-apocalyptic: it's a road designed for a lot of people, but with no people on it. Graffiti spanned most of the abandoned buildings that butted up to the highway's sound barrier walls.

As we approached the exit for Woodward Avenue all my teenage memories came flooding back. At nineteen I had spent countless nights in the most amazing jazz clubs in Detroit with musical friends who even performed in them sometimes. Memories of laughing and dancing in Saint Andrews Hall, my favorite nightclub, filled my mind. I remembered driving on Saturday nights in my friend Jason's enormous Chevy diesel pickup—it made all the cars within a twenty-foot radius vibrate. We would descend into the Windsor tunnel to make our way to Canada for another dance party. As I reflected on that time, I was full of joy and grief. I missed my innocence, my sense of wonder, and the spontaneity of life in those days. I missed the feeling I had had that my life was going to be extraordinary. During my time in Northern California I'd been on a destructive rinse-and-repeat cycle for years and I was still slowly crawling out of it. But I had been capable of happiness, once. It was a thought that pulled me forward but whenever I think of moving back to Michigan, I stop myself. I treasure and hold my memories with great reverence. Living there wouldn't be the same. Aspects of my teenage years had been happy, full of wonder and possibility, a gauge for what I know it's possible for me to feel. Not enough to peg a life on.

Dad found a parking spot quickly in front of the DIA, bought our tickets, and we went straight for the photography: Bruce Weber's pictures of people around Detroit. My favorite photo was of Asia Newson, a girl who became an entrepreneur at a very young age. The thoughts I had just had about my own innocence were shining so brightly all over her face, and there was a powerful beauty emanating from her. I thought, *I remember that girl. I know she is still alive inside me somewhere. How do I find her again?* Tears rolled down my face.

The caption read: The spirit of Detroit is all wrapped up in Asia Newson, the city's youngest entrepreneur, who aspires to be America's first rapping president.

Good for you girl, don't ever let anyone take that inspiration away from you. I wanted to tell her: *protect your heart, your gifts, and your dreams. The Erlkönig[1] will come after you, he got me many years ago. Hold your dreams close and be aware, you can outrun him if you're smart. You must know yourself; you must remember who you are: a powerful being with unlimited potential.*

We entered a huge gallery room where *Detroit's Industry*, the Diego Rivera series of frescos, are painted. They were so beautiful, the energy of them took my breath away. Dad proceeded to tell me what each panel meant, frame by frame. He knew every story behind the figures. I couldn't believe it. Dad knew about art?! I felt horrible; how did I not know this? Dad was a very proud man. He loved Detroit and he adored Michigan. He had worked for the Ford Motor Company for thirty-five years and thought the auto industry was more than just the fabric of the American culture: it was the holy grail of liberties. His family had been Polish and Irish farmers who had lived in southeastern Michigan for generations—simple but hearty folk. They had struggled for what they had earned in life and there was nothing highbrow about them. So, it was especially poetic to hear Dad speak about the paintings. I remember how it felt to be in that room with him, sharing an intimate moment of appreciation for something beautiful. Dad showed me a side of himself that had been invisible to me before. I was giddy. We moved on through the museum looking at paintings that I didn't understand, artifacts from ancient cultures and old jousting suits. Dad and I joked at how uncomfortable and heavy they must have been. How would you go pee?

------

[1] The Erlkönig is an evil elf in European folk tales who preys upon children.

We finished at the museum and drove down to the end of Woodward Avenue. We walked through Hart Plaza to the Detroit River looking over to Canada, listened to the creak of the historic and dilapidated Boblo Boat bobbing in the water, and read the Gateway to Freedom plaque together:

> *Until Emancipation, Detroit and the Detroit River community served as the gateway to freedom for thousands of African American people escaping enslavement. Detroit was one of the largest terminals of the Underground Railroad, a network of abolitionists aiding enslaved people seeking freedom. Detroit's Underground Railroad code name was Midnight. At first, Michigan was a destination for freedom seekers, but Canada became a safer sanctuary after slavery was abolished there in 1834. With passage of the Fugitive Slave Act in 1850, many runaways left their homes in Detroit and crossed the river to Canada to remain free. Some returned after Emancipation in 1863.*
>
> *The successful operation of Detroit's Underground Railroad was due to the effort and cooperation of diverse groups of people including people of African descent, Whites, and North American Indians. This legacy of freedom is a vital part of Detroit and its history.*

Tears and emotion welled up inside. I could feel why Dad loved this place so much. Despite Detroit's problems through the years, a palpable pulse runs through the landscape, an authenticity and realness that I have never encountered anywhere else. My chest sank as I realized how a place so brilliant and special was being left for ruin amidst poor government and a failing auto industry. But what I also felt was resilience.

Before the world's fair started spotlighting world cities, and while automobile factories were still merely concepts on paper, Detroit had held its own fair—the Detroit International Exposition and Fair—in 1889. At that time Michigan's primary asset was agriculture and civic leaders wanted to reveal to the world her varied manufacturing economy. The city produced shoes, soap, paints and varnishes, hoopskirts, patent medicines, railroad cars, and packaged seeds, among many other products. When the automobile companies took up residence many of those commodities were overshadowed. Currently there is a flurry of a new generation of handmade goods being created and manufactured in Detroit. I was delighted to find out that a new American-made watch company called Shinola is bringing back a trade and a craftsmanship that is greatly needed.

I've always marveled at Detroit's architecture: the city has one of the largest surviving collections of late nineteenth and early twentieth-century buildings in the United States. The city is home to huge turn-of-the-century mansions filled with cherry wood handrails and stained-glass windows—a friend of mine was proud to purchase one of these antique windows after high school. The city boasts an eclectic blend of styles and many of the buildings are now registered historical landmarks. You can find art deco, ornate Beaux-Arts facades, Victorian commercial buildings, even a rare building from the Antebellum period at 1244 Randolf Street built in 1840. I can go on and on, but it seems that every type of architecture can be found and explored here.

Dad and I looped back over to the Spirit of Detroit sculpture, which has always inspired within me a feeling of hope. I find it deeply moving but the only way to know its wisdom is in perfect silence. I wanted to stand there for hours.

Unfortunately, I had a plane to catch. We proceeded on to the central square in the city's renewed downtown area to find it was full of street vendors and music. We grabbed some coffee at a very new and chic coffee bar. I had heard that Detroit was having some sort of renaissance, but I was delighted and surprised at what I saw. Gentrification was definitely unfolding at full throttle, at least in the downtown area. The streets were filled with new restaurants, outdoor cafes, and a huge farmers' market. A shiny Comerica Park served as a backdrop for the new downtown. A gaggle of twenty- to-thirty-something white kids wearing name badges flaunting a tech company flooded the sidewalks. I assumed they were staying at a nearby hotel for a conference. Perhaps the grit of the city was still there somewhere, under the glitter.

As Dad and I walked and laughed and talked together, I took photos of protestors demanding that the city pay for their water, and all the new buildings. It was such a pleasure and honor to spend this time with him. I was proud that he was my dad. I got to feel what a hard worker he was, how his sensitivity and kindness showed up as naïveté and sweetness. I was starting to see beyond my childhood resentments toward him. He was not perfect. But he had a lot of positive qualities, and that visit was destined to crystallize into a magical memory I was to hold onto forever. One last visit. One last opportunity to connect. And I had no idea at the time we were on a collision course with my last chance to tell him how much he had meant to me.

CHAPTER 3

THE CALL

May 25, 2015

I went home to California, after our summer visit, feeling the grace made peace with my dad and at least shared some of my vulnerabilities with my mother. I had been twenty when I moved to San Diego in 1996, bringing to fruition the dreams I'd had of living near the beach since visiting California with my parents when I'd been five years old. I moved from San Diego north to the San Francisco Bay area in 2003 and had been living there ever since.

Nearly a year had passed since my landmark visit with my parents and life had gone on pretty much as it always did. I had talked to dad on Sunday knowing that he was declining and the phone rang two days later.

"Yeah, Dad is in the hospital," my mom said in her typically flat, detached southern, "everything-is-fine" tone. "I found him slumped over on the couch. He was turning purple. I got him on the floor and did CPR until the ambulance came. They took him down the street to Garden City Hospital." Those were the facts.

My mind started racing and my heart began to pound. I'd known this was coming but when I had talked to my dad the previous evening I thought I had at least a few weeks to get used to the ebbing of his life. This was too soon!

"How long was he unconscious?" I asked.

"I don't know," Mom said. "I'd left the room to go work on the computer. I was gone for probably forty-five minutes or so. It was real quiet. Dad wasn't coughing, so I went in and there he was."

Dad had been coughing for weeks, and he had been in and out of the hospital for a variety of reasons and with a variety of infections for the past eleven years. He was all hacked up from the surgeries done to take care of his cancer and Mom thought this was another one of those times when the doctors would take care of the infection and send him home.

I think if I'd been living in Michigan his cancer would have impacted me more but being so far away, I felt detached. I had never been part of his care—hadn't gone to the hospital or his medical appointments with him—and shortly after he was diagnosed with cancer, I started drinking so I was also mired in my own dysfunction. I didn't have the capacity to care for anybody else. I was just trying to make it through life and the fact that I'd been hearing about the routine of infection, treatment, surgery, and recovery for so long also meant there was an air of "new normal" about his health. But this time was different. I don't know how I knew. Sometimes I have insights and premonitions that are spot on target. The cold claw of anxiety started crawling up my back.

"Should I come home?" I asked.

"No, he'll be fine. The doctor is running tests and will call in the morning."

"Okay. Did you call Aunt Pat?" Aunt Pat is Dad's younger sister and his best friend. He told her everything, and she knew more than anybody about my father, his life, and his health.

"No, not yet. I'll call her in a minute."

"Are you going to the hospital?"

"No, I'll go in the morning."

The image of Dad being alone all night by himself broke my heart. I called Aunt Pat to see if she would go over and keep him company.

The next day, Tuesday, I got up early to go to my office. I'd been practicing acupuncture for sixteen years by this point and I had a full day ahead of me. It was beyond difficult to stay focused. I called Aunt Pat in the afternoon.

"Your dad hasn't regained consciousness," she said. "The doctors have him surrounded with ice packs to mitigate any damage that could have been done to his nervous system. They're running more tests, but they don't know anything yet."

I called Mom, too, but she didn't answer the phone. I left a message but didn't expect to hear back. She rarely returned my calls. For most of the day I debated whether I should buy a plane ticket and head home. One more day, I kept thinking. I'll give it one more day.

On Wednesday I drove to the teaching gig in Berkeley I'd had for the previous eight years. The nagging pit in my stomach continued to grow; it was undeniable that something was really wrong. *Still unconscious, fuck. Will we ever have another conversation?* I arrived at school and started my 8:30 a.m. shift. Ninety minutes later, Aunt Pat called.

"It doesn't look good, hun. You need to come right away." That's all she needed to say. I burst into tears in the school clinic, surrounded by acupuncture interns and supervisors. Everyone was alarmed, asking me if I was okay. I shook my head and ran into the clinic dean's office. I could barely speak.

"What's happening?" Mike asked.

After a few moments I was able to whisper, "My dad is dying."

"Go home, I'll cover your shift. Don't worry about anything, just go."

My co-worker and friend, Christine, came into his office. I stood up and collapsed in her arms. All I could think was *wait for me Dad, I'm on my way, please wait for me to say goodbye.* I walked out into the clinic room and a dozen people stared at me in concern. I announced that my dad was dying, and I needed to go.

My internal world had started to unravel and was coming crashing down. I couldn't focus enough to purchase a plane ticket, and I couldn't hear what other people were saying to me. I dialed my good friend, Georgia.

"Honeywabbit! How's my honeywabbit?" she asked in a light voice.

All I could do was cry.

"Honeywabbit what's going on?"

Breathless, I said, "Dad's in the hospital. He's dying. Please come to my house and help me."

"Okay, leaving now."

Berkeley is thirty minutes from my home in Lagunitas. I could barely drive and have no idea how I made it home. I was crying and shaking the whole way. *Dad, wait for me. Wait for me, please.* I couldn't bear the thought of missing the chance to say goodbye, of seeing him just one more time.

I got home and started throwing clothes in a suitcase, not knowing if anything even matched. Was it summer or winter? What do I pack? Do I need to bring any legal documents? Fuck I can't even think. Denial and shock are a rough combination. I felt like I was drugged. I'd been following a spiritual path for quite some time by this point and had gathered some powerful tools to support me when the walls of my world started to lean and crumble. Meditation. Energy work. Yoga. Breath work. And more. But when crisis struck, there was no time, no bandwidth to stop, pause, and reset my nervous system. I was in a total fight-or-flight reaction mode, and I couldn't think let alone gather the grace to support myself. Georgia walked in ten minutes later and embraced me.

"It's going to be okay, honeywabbit. God will take care of you. I'll take care of you. Whatever you need." Her hugs always calmed me down. She had a softness and gentleness about her that could disarm Godzilla. Our friendship has gently faded into my past over the years that followed, as many of my friendships have, but I will be forever grateful for her support in that very heartsick time.

By the time I finished packing, Georgia had found me a ticket. I called Aunt Pat.

"I want to go straight to the hospital when I get there," I said.

"I don't think they allow visitation at that time but let me see what I can do," she said.

"Okay, Auntie, see you soon."

The time could not go fast enough. I tried to distract myself by watching movies on the flight, but tears kept streaming down my face. When I thought I couldn't cry anymore, more tears came. Finally, the sweet music of the flight attendant's voice came over the intercom.

"We are starting our descent into Detroit. Please bring your seat and tray tables to an upright position. We will be landing shortly. Temperature in Detroit is a balmy 73 degrees and local time is 11:15 p.m. Welcome to Detroit."

Some welcome.

CHAPTER 4

DETROIT

May 27, 2015

That word, "balmy," flooded my mind with memories and for a moment I felt joy. The thing I miss most about Michigan are the warm nights when I could run fearlessly around town with friends in tank tops, laughing. Bay Area nights are cool if not cold; there is no wearing of tank tops. Those teenage summer nights are so forward in my mind they seem like they happened yesterday. I can taste and feel them when I close my eyes. It's nature at her most sultry, most mysterious, when the whole world is ripe with possibility.

As we taxied to the gate I called Uncle Steve, who was going to pick me up from Detroit's Metropolitan Airport.

"Hey honey," he answered.

"Hi Uncle, I should be on the curb in thirty. I'll call you when I'm there."

"Okay, honey. We can go to the hospital. The doctors are expecting you."

They're expecting me? This cannot be good.

My bag came quickly, and I went out to the curb. Oh God ... the air. I took a deep breath and exhaled. It felt like the first time I'd breathed all day. Uncle pulled up, got out and gave me a hug, then he put my bags in the car. As we drove away from the airport towards the hospital he grabbed my hand.

"It's not good, hun."

"I felt this was coming last week. I talked to Dad three times on the phone. I knew on Sunday. But it doesn't make it any easier."

We rode on and he joked a little about the car being a mess and then said some things about my cousins, Audra and Kelly. I was slightly tuned out. Then he asked me point blank.

"Do you want to drink?"

Up until that moment I had forgotten I was a recovering alcoholic. I had just picked up my three-year chip a few weeks earlier. We always talked about these kinds of moments in AA, the ones that caused people to relapse. Like other people in recovery there are years of my life when I was so checked out I have no memories of what I did, who I was with, or how I felt. The truth is, I didn't start drinking until I was twenty-six and living in California. I had gone to acupuncture school which introduced me to the self-realization movement, and I began doing yoga, going to therapy, and meditating. I'd been dedicated and focused for years, holding together in the aftermath of a childhood and adolescence that ranged from unhappy to downright abusive, and then life fell apart. My friends all moved away, I got into a dysfunctional relationship, I became engaged to someone and then broke up with him, a business I had planned with friends fell apart before it got started, a close friend died, I couldn't get work in my field, and then, having found a job at a bookstore, I just said, "Fuck it, I'm going to have fun." Meditation, discipline, and hard work, didn't heal me, didn't bring me relief or peace. While I had brief moments of feeling whole and complete, I mostly felt like I was treading water. There'd been no significant permanent shift in my emotional state or wholeness. I was lonely, unhappy, and in emotional pain. I wanted to forget. And so, I did. I had one friend in particular who introduced me to cocaine and other party drugs, and I began to drink heavily and constantly. I became dark and depressed, and later in my drinking, blackouts became a way of life for me. I couldn't remember anything. I overdosed once and came close to meeting my Maker but didn't. The truth was, I didn't actually care if I lived or died.

Finally, after eleven years of risky, alcohol-fueled behavior I woke up after a night of partying with a friend and realized I couldn't remember anything about the previous night ... but my parked car nestled into the side of a hill showed evidence that I had put my friend's life in serious danger.

You've got a problem, I said to myself. That day I reached out to a friend who I knew was sober and I started going to AA. I had shared my history of addiction with my Uncle Steve and Aunt Pat so, my uncle's question about whether I wanted a drink or not was pertinent.

"No, haven't even thought about it," I replied, and felt gratitude washing over me. I could go through this experience, totally present, and not even have a single thought of wanting to drink. A miracle.

"That's great," Uncle Steve said. "I'm so proud of you." I was proud of me, too.

And I was exhausted. It was close to midnight when we got to Garden City Hospital Emergency entrance and went through security. Uncle guided me down a long hallway to the elevator. The hospital was very quiet and peaceful.

The doors opened onto the second floor. We walked down a short hallway and turned left into the ICU. To my right, two nurses said hello from the nurses' station. I figured they guessed who I was. There were no other visitors. Dad was at the end of the hallway. Each room had three walls, with a curtain facing the hallway in front. A nurse sitting outside at a small table stood up when she saw me.

"You must be Heather."

As she said it, I looked into the room and saw Dad lying there with what looked like hundreds of tubes coming out of every part of his body. I was stunned. I was not expecting him to look like that. My heart sank. He's on life support; no one told me. I have Medical Power of Attorney. I'm the one who will decide when to turn off these machines. The realization hit me square in the heart. I walked over to Dad and started sobbing again.

"Dad, I'm here," I whispered in his ear. "Thank you so much for waiting for me. I love you more than you will ever know." I sat on the edge of the bed and held his hand. Uncle was chatting with the nurse, but I didn't hear what they were saying. All I could do was stare at my dad. He was cold, his body rigid. They had him packed in ice to slow down any brain damage. This was not my father.

The doctor came in. "Hello, Heather," he said, introducing himself.

"What happened?"

"We aren't exactly sure. There is no sign of a heart attack or stroke. We are running more tests."

Dad had been in the hospital two full days, and they still didn't know what was wrong with him. My legs were weak; I wanted to get to my parents' house and sleep. I knew tomorrow would be a long day. I gave my father's hand a squeeze and walked out of the room. Uncle drove me to my parent's house in Redford, just a few blocks away. As we pulled up, Mom opened the door.

"Yeah, hello." She was wearing the uniform she had lived in, day in and day out for as long as I could remember: blue sweatpants, a plain blue cotton T-shirt, and a little navy-blue visor she was so attached to that she sometimes slept in it. As I stood there, I noticed an unusual smell, and with horror, realized it was Mom. She must not have washed her clothes in a week. I studied her more closely. The inner legs of her sweatpants had holes in them, and so did her T-shirt.

"Hi Mom." I gave her an awkward hug, half holding my breath. "I have to go to bed. Goodnight." There was only so much I could deal with at any one time. My mother was beyond my limit for that day

CHAPTER 5

ENTERING THE SURREAL

I dragged my baggage to my room and snuck out to the back-yard to smoke a cigarette. I'd hid this addiction for twenty years, and it was the one thing I had not told my parents about during my confession a year earlier. I looked out into the yard and inhaled deeply, feeling the calming fingers of the nicotine slide through my lungs and ease my nervous system off high alert. I thought Mom had gone back to bed, but she came outside to join me. Shit.

"What are you doing out here?"

"Smoking."

"When did you start that?"

"When I was nineteen."

"How come you never told us?"

"I didn't want to disappoint Dad."

"Oh. Well, just don't put the butts in the garden." She went back inside. Not the reaction I thought I would get. She had always gotten in my face about using drugs and smoking as a kid, to scare me away from it, I suppose. I knew my mom had been a smoker when she was younger—everybody was in the 1940s and 1950s in the American South—but she had quit when I was born. When I was a student at Western Michigan University, I worked part-time at a coffee shop where everyone smoked. One of my co-workers said I was a goodie-two shoes. I was boring. I needed more fun in my life. I was shocked— I'd never thought of myself as boring, quite the contrary. *Me, boring? Are you kidding?* I started smoking so as not to feel so square and to maintain the bad girl image I had of myself. But I had also been in a very vulnerable state at the time—I was homesick, I had two roommates who were "mean girls," and I was not doing well in school—and I found that smoking eased my self-hatred, my profound feelings of grief; it took the edge off. I didn't feel so hopeless.

I stood outside looking up at the stars, taking deep breaths, letting the stillness of the night wash over my trembling body. Calm down. Breathe. Calm down. I felt myself going into emotional paralysis. Entering the realm of the surreal. I finished my smoke and went back inside to take a shower. Somehow, I managed to fall asleep.

I woke up at 6:00 the next morning, full of anxiety. The plan was to drive Dad's car over for breakfast with Aunt Pat, Uncle Steve, and my cousin, Audra, at a diner on Plymouth Road. Just six months earlier, Dad had bought a fully loaded three-year-old Ford Explorer. Being a Ford family, Dad had driven Explorers for years, but never one this new. It was his pride and joy. He loved this vehicle. It had a dark blue exterior and a tan leather interior—the Eddie Bauer model. I got in the driver's seat. It smelled like him, and I could feel him driving it. A plastic bag for garbage hung on the fastener of the glove box, and there were napkins in the console along with dental floss and a bottle of water. Dad never went anywhere without water and somehow seeing them—items he had touched perhaps just a few days earlier—added to the surreal feeling that this was all a dream. In the backseat was a black bag that carried a roll of toilet paper (for some reason) and the lunch he hadn't eaten – a now-moldy cheese sandwich and an apple.

As I was driving, I tuned in to my body to get a sense of how I was feeling—numbness in my limbs and my mind was expanding, but my heart was alive with feelings of gratitude for my family, especially Aunt Pat. We would walk through this together; I wasn't totally alone, or so I thought. I arrived at the diner and saw a cream-colored Volkswagen in the parking lot. They were already here. The diner seemed to be a hundred years old, with a weathered wood facade, faded from decades of cold, harsh winters and hot, humid summers. It was not a place I would usually ever eat, having become so spoiled in the Bay Area with quite possibly the freshest and best food in the country. I walked in and the smell of rancid oil and old cleaning rags filled the air. I wasn't very hungry to begin with but now I felt nauseous. I hugged my uncle and auntie and slid down the brown vinyl seat, past huge holes where the stuffing was coming out. We sat in silence for a few moments, trying to come up with idle chit chat so we could seem normal. Audra arrived and broke the silence.

"Hey Heather, great to see you. Too bad it's under these circumstances."

"Great to see you too. Feels good to be home." Audra talked about the drama in her life. She always had funny stories to share about her two kids, the family's Great Dane, and her small backyard farm of chickens, rabbits, and a gigantic turtle appropriately named Tiny. It felt good to laugh, to take my mind off the inevitable.

We finished eating and walked outside. The day was warm and the humid air enveloped me like a blanket filled with freshly cut grass and flowers—familiar smells of my childhood. And then we drove to see Dad. Entering the hospital, the sound of chatter gave me some sense of normality. We got off the elevator at the second floor and walked down the long hallway. Turning the corner into the ICU, I could see the patients' curtains open, and the nurses coming and going.

"Hello, Heather," the nurses called. I arrived at Dad's room to find a nurse next to his bed, tending to him. It was a great relief to know he was never alone. Nurses were by his side all day and night.

"Hi Heather, I'm Michelle."

"Any change?" I asked.

"No, I'm sorry. I'm going to get the doctor to come talk to you."

"Okay."

I looked at Dad in disbelief. *Was this really the end?* I sat next to him and grabbed his hand. It was swollen—I assumed from all the IV fluids—and was now very warm, like he was running a fever. It didn't look like his hand. None of it looked like him. His eyes were big and swollen, there was a tube coming from his mouth, and IVs in both arms. His chest was rising and falling with a hardness and a force that seemed unnatural; his feet were covered in big socks. *What was actually happening to him?* I stood up and leaned over to kiss his head, "I love you so much, Dad. Thanks for waiting."

The doctor arrived and introduced himself. "Hi, I'm Dr. Ruettinger. You must be Heather." I wasn't interested in formalities.

"What happened to my dad?"

"We don't know exactly. We ran tests and there is no indication of a heart attack or stroke, but his heart is not working properly. We put him on ice to slow down the inflammation and any damage that might have been caused due to lack of circulation."

He checked Dad's eye reflexes with a pen light.

"Unfortunately, he doesn't have any reflexes, an indication that there is very little brain function, and his heart cannot pump on its own. See this machine?" He pointed to a small box next to Dad's bed. "This is serving as his heart."

"So, there is nothing more you can do? Are you saying Dad is basically on life support?"

"Yes, that's what I'm saying. You have medical power of attorney and the power to sign the Do Not Resuscitate (DNR), order right?"

"Yes, I do."

"Let me go get that paperwork."

Sitting there I felt so alone and very small. Even though I knew Dad's wishes—he wanted no extraordinary measures, no far-fetched interventions—the idea that I had to make the ulti-mate decision to end his life was unbearable. Me, his daughter. Why not Mom or Aunt Pat or Aunt Mary? He chose me. I turned to Aunt Pat, wanting her to make the decision for me.

"Is this the right decision? Should we wait longer?"

"There is nothing more the doctors can do. Ken didn't want to linger, we all know that." The doctor came back with the legal paperwork. I signed Dad's life away with my signature on pages that I couldn't read; my brain was barely functioning.

"Okay," said the doctor. "Would you like to terminate now?"

What?

"NO!"

It was only 9:00 a.m. Regardless of what anyone else wanted, I was going to spend the day with Dad. I would also have to get Mom back to the hospital somehow. In her mind,

Dad was going to wake up and come back home like he always did, and life would go on as usual.

We decided to reconvene at 6:30 that evening.

As I drove back home, my heart was pounding. *How am I going to get Mom out of the house to go see Dad? Would she think I was lying? Go into some story about how he was going to be fine?* An uncomfortable anxiety was building.

As I turned into my parents' neighborhood I was reminded again of the simple pleasures of summer. I passed some kids playing in sprinklers in their front yards, a pair of joggers out with their puppies, and some folks out on their porches drinking beer, watching the day go by. For a moment I forgot why I was there.

I pulled into the driveway and noticed the pit in my stomach I had temporarily forgotten. I went inside and sat down. Dad's fifty-four-inch TV was blaring conservative commentator Glenn Beck's program, and Mom was in the kitchen making something. I waited for her to come into the family room.

"Well, what did the doctor say?" she asked.

"Doesn't look good, Mom. You need to come to the hospital and say goodbye." She looked at me in disbelief. Leaving the house was one of the things that triggered Mom's episodes. It usually activated her paranoia. She would start saying that she was being followed and refuse to budge.

"Really? He isn't coming home? I thought this was just another infection, that they would just give him antibiotics and he would be home in a couple of weeks."

"I wish that were the case, but no. He has no brain function, and his heart isn't beating on its own." I watched closely for Mom's reaction, my body clenching and waiting for some cockamamie story, anticipating that I would have to scream and yell and pull out my "big guns." But to my surprise, she sat there for a few moments, silently processing what I had said.

"Okay, let me get my things." It was a small miracle.

As I watched her get up, my heart broke. I could see that she was preparing herself as best she could, and I could also see the child in her, the one that Dad had taken care of my whole life. *She is totally alone now, she won't be able to manage life on her own*, I thought.

"I'm ready to go," Mom said.

"Do you want to drive?"

"I can't see." She was still wearing a pair of my glasses from high school, as she refused to leave the house to see an eye doctor to get her own. The places where they had broken over the years had been patched together with scotch tape and paperclips. I assumed she just needed new glasses.

"What do you mean you can't see?"

"I haven't been able to see out of my right eye for years now."

"What? Why haven't you gone to the eye doctor?" I looked at her eye. It was completely cloudy. "You have cataracts, Mom. You can get surgery, and they can fix that easily."

"There isn't any money. I don't have insurance."

That was true. For some reason that I will never know, Dad never got health insurance for Mom. Physically, she was a mess, blind in her right eye, half blind in her left, and with only one bottom tooth remaining. The rest of her teeth had fallen out over the years, and paranoia prevented her from seeing any doctor or dentist: she believed she was being followed everywhere she went.

Back in the ICU, Michelle greeted us.

"Hi Heather. I've been sitting here the last two days thinking, 'does this man have any family?' There haven't been many people in to see him."

"Hi Michelle, this is my mom, Susan. The word is just getting out, so there should be more folks coming in to say goodbye."

"Oh, good. Hi Susan." She offered a handshake, but Mom recoiled.

"Oh, I have stuff on my hands." This was a lie. Her words were barely intelligible. She was terrified of people.

I was starting to get a feeling of impending doom.

I sat down on Dad's left side, Mom on his right. She was uncomfortable, fidgeting with his blankets and tubes. I watched as her tears flowed, and she told him he was a great man. Then we just sat in silence and watched Dad breathe.

After an hour or so I took Mom home and came back on my own. Finally, just the two of us. I was cycling through sadness, grief, shock, and numbness, recycle-repeat. I leaned over, kissed his head, and rested my cheek there. My mind wandered, reflecting on our lifelong relationship.

CHAPTER 6

THIRTY-NINE YEARS

When I was a very little girl I had idolized my dad. Whatever he was doing, I wanted to do. I worked on cars, mowed the lawn, shoveled snow. He always had time for me. When I asked him to play with me, which was every day, he did. He took the training wheels off my bicycle in the backyard. He held on to the back, running alongside with me as I pedaled my little five-year-old legs so fast.

"Okay Heather, keep pedaling!" I pedaled as fast as I could.

"Okay, Daddy you can let go!" I yelled.

"I already did." I could hear him laughing. For the last five seconds I had been riding on my own. Exhilaration and excitement filled me, I was ecstatic. I stood up, turned the bike around and rode back to him. We were both grinning from ear to ear.

"I did it!"

"You sure did!"

We would garden together and play softball catch. He showed me how to take photographs. The first picture I took was of a hot air balloon. He drove me to dance and swim lessons nearly every day, picked up a whole carload of kids and took us to the movies almost every weekend; he took me clothes shopping on a regular basis. On Saturdays I would wake up early and watch cartoons, eagerly waiting for Dad to get home from

Ford—Dad, worked midnights—so we could go to Big Boy and order strawberry waffles. I would color and Dad would read the newspaper, his attention broken up by my giggles and silly rantings. It was like this until I turned eleven or so. As I recalled these things, I realized something deep within that took my breath away. He had never said "no" to me. He worked fifty to sixty hours a week. When he could have been sleeping, he was meeting my needs in those early years.

I felt his sacrifice, his love, his adoration for me.

Oh my God. I felt so much shame; I'd been so painfully selfish.

When I became a pre-teen, my relationship with him shifted radically. He worked so much that he wasn't around a lot, much to my mother's wrath. That had started when I was 8 or so, this time of my life is very blurry. She would get in my face multiple times a week, intense with anger.

"I'm being followed, and you know who's doing it. Things that only you and your father know are being spoken to me in the grocery store, and elsewhere. You are ruining my life!" she would shout. If I protested at all, she would point her finger and hiss at me. "You would be a great actress because you are such a good liar."

One of the first times she spoke to me like this, I was so terrified I wet my pants, ran to my room and hid under the bed. My early response was always to shut down with fear but as the years went by I became as angry as a banshee at the consistent violation of boundaries and lack of care towards my wellbeing.

Her rantings went on like this for years and I never spoke a word of it to Dad. I thought it was my fault that Mom was so angry and crazy. I internalized all of it, and by the time I got to high school I was drowning in self-loathing and hatred for everyone and everything. My attitude was horrible.

Coping meant I had to shut everyone out, including Dad.

By my mid-twenties, we had become more estranged. Dad was increasingly judgmental about the choices I was making, especially around finances. There came a point in my late twenties when I didn't speak to him for two years because I couldn't bear listening to his disapproval. He never expressed pride about the things I had accomplished, like moving 3,000 miles away at the age of twenty, earning a master's degree in Chinese medicine, or moving to New York by myself—or even just the fact that I had been independent for years. Resentment, frustration, and anger created an impenetrable wall that lasted for almost eighteen years. I was desperately wanting to let go of it. It was suffocating the joy from my life.

I understood why he had acted the way he did. His father had died suddenly of a heart attack when Dad was eleven, and it had devastated him. I can't imagine growing up without a father. He was overcompensating, wanting to help me because he hadn't had a father to guide him through his own life. But his judgement didn't help me, it was hurting me.

Sitting with him in the ICU, I felt free of our past. None of it mattered. I leaned over and whispered in his ear,

"Dad, I love you so much. You are the most amazing father and I'm so proud to be your daughter. Your work ethic inspires me. You never let cancer or anything else stop you from living your life or fulfilling your duties. You kept marching forward, living with integrity, and standing firm in your truth. You wanted to work 'til the day you died, and that is exactly what you did. I have no unfinished business, Dad, whatever of the past I was holding on to has vanished. I only see and feel unconditional love, me for you and you for me. What a miracle it is we get to have this rare moment together. I hope you feel how much I love you."

I fell on his chest and sobbed.

I lay on him and sat by his side for a couple of hours. Just him and me, surrounded by the sound of the machines keeping him alive.

I could feel that Dad was tired. I sensed his sadness and regret, wishing that his life could have been different, that Mom wasn't sick. I would never know exactly what he desired in life, but I knew he wasn't totally fulfilled. He had been a bit of a wild young man when he had been younger. He liked fast cars and drinking with his friends and I learned from my aunts that he could have had any woman he wanted. As a Ford employee, at one point he had been sent to Southern California to test drive cars in the desert. One of his co-workers, Buzzy, had a cousin and he set the two of them up on a blind date. They went to the Hollywood Bowl to see Joe Cocker, and my dad thought this cousin was the most beautiful woman he had ever seen. She had an hourglass figure and long black hair and when his four-month assignment in California was over, he said, "Why don't you come back to Michigan with me?" They got married and soon I came along.

Dad often told Mom she had saved his life because he stopped drinking like an idiot when she came into his life. He did stupid things when he was under the influence—drove his car too fast, rode galloping horses backwards ... it's as though when Mom showed up, he had a reason to care a little more about his life.

For her part, Mom came from a poor family in Mississippi, and her mother had been verbally abusive to her. The combination of being young and unsupported as a new mother did not do Mom's mental state any favors and Dad's carefree life had disappeared the second I arrived. I have strong memories of my parents arguing a lot and I know Dad disappeared into his own life, working overtime at Ford and acquiring investment properties so he had increased responsibilities to keep him from being home. He pretty much left me to deal with Mom and her increasing weirdness on my own. I'm sure that's not what he had planned for his life. Our lives. There was no do-over. And now he was ebbing away from us. In that moment life seemed impossibly short.

CHAPTER 7

SAYING GOODBYE

May 28, 2015

I was content with the time I had spent with Dad, so I went home to eat a late lunch and get some rest. When I'm stressed my digestion turns off, so I only managed to take a couple of bites of a sandwich that turned in my stomach. I laid my head on my pillow and closed my eyes.

When I woke up it was 4:00 p.m. and Mom was zoning out in front of the TV.

"I'm going back to the hospital. I'll be back at 6:15 to pick you up," I said.

"Okay," she said, her eyes fixed on the screen.

When I got to Dad's room there were three attractive women in their late-thirties-to-mid-forties there, all crying and touching or holding some part of my father. They worked with Dad at the bus yard—where he played out his Second Act career—and although I appreciated the emotional impact my father's impending death was having on them, it was a bizarre sight. After Dad retired from Ford he couldn't stand sitting around. He had a few different odd jobs until he found his second love: driving a school bus. He loved driving that bus and being of service. Dad was always a ladies' man and had incredible charm. I walked up and introduced myself.

"Hi, I'm Heather, Ken's daughter."

"Oh hello!" They each introduced themselves.

"I've heard so much about you."

"Your father adored you."

"Yes, you're all he ever talked about."

My heart broke more deeply. They stayed for a few more minutes. The nurse, Michelle, was there.

"You know, after how quiet it's been, I'm so happy to see everyone stopping by today, to feel the love they have for your father. It feels like I know him." Tears started rolling down her face. "This will be difficult for me. He is a very special man."

Dozens of people had come to see Dad that day. There was so much love in the air. In his older years, he had a way of spreading joy everywhere he went; you could see it in people's eyes, how deeply he touched people's hearts just by being himself.

And then it was just Dad and me again. I wanted more time with him by myself before 6:15 came, holding his hand, touching his skin. I studied every piece of his body. I touched his face, brushed his hair, examined his huge Polish eyes, laid my head on his chest one more time so I could feel his heartbeat and his breath, felt the muscles of his arms, legs, and feet. I didn't want to forget anything about him.

Michelle came in to change his IV.

"Okay, Ken. I'm changing your IV now. It will just take a second. We're going to replace this old bandage too."

I appreciated her warmth towards Dad and how she talked to him as if he were awake. She had done various things to him throughout the day while I had been there, always talking to him.

"I'm going to wet your lips with some water—they're getting dry and cracking a bit."

Dad chose the best way to go. No drama, no suffering, no lengthy hospital stays. He was done.

I had been shocked to learn earlier in the day from Aunt Pat that during one of Dad's checkups the previous year, the doctor had told him that his cancer had come back aggressively in his remaining kidney. At some point, he would need daily, in-home dialysis sessions every four hours, each one lasting between thirty and sixty minutes. He wouldn't be strong enough for the regular four-hour outpatient treatments most people undergo three times a week.

"There's no way in hell I'm going to do that," he had confided to Aunt Pat. "I'll die before that happens." No one else had known about his prognosis.

I wish I had known. I would have come home at least one more time.

It's not surprising to me that the doctors couldn't find the exact reason Dad's heart stopped. I believe there came a moment when Dad just reached up to God and said, "I'm ready."

When it was approaching 6:00 p.m. I left to go get Mom. When we got back, everyone was already at Dad's side. Aunt Pat, Uncle Steve, Audra, Kelly, Dad's other sister, Mary, her husband, Jim, and my cousin Megan. My heart started beating fast and hard. For a few moments I thought I would pass out. Everyone took turns saying goodbye and telling stories, laughing between the tears. Kelly told us about her party on Saturday. Dad couldn't make it during the day because he had to drive the girls' basketball team to a game. He finally showed up for the party at 9:00 p.m., knocking, and calling, "Anybody home?" Ordinarily it would have been unusual for Dad to go out so late. I know he knew his time was coming. I loved him even more for his awareness.

It was nearing 8:00 p.m. and we were all tired and ready for our final farewell. A nurse went to get the doctor. We stepped out so Michelle could remove tubes and other devices, explaining to Dad in detail what she was doing all the while. After she finished, we gathered around him. I sat on the edge of the bed, holding both of his hands.

"I love you Dad, it's okay to go. I love you so much."

I kept repeating it as we all watched the clock. We were told that once the life support was stopped, he would die within minutes. We heard that horrible death rattle in the back of his throat. After fifteen minutes of it, Aunt Pat said she couldn't bear staying any longer and listening to that sound. It was clear Dad wasn't ready to go just yet. I had to chuckle inside because that was so typical of him. Defying natural law, making life—and death—on his own terms.

Finally, just Mom and I remained. I could see her beginning to slip into an episode, even as she kept repeating the Lord's prayer, touching Dad, and saying what a great man he was. I watched her as she transformed. Her eyes emptied out in a combination of absence and possession. It scared me and I shuddered, the ghost of my old childhood fear of her behavior starting to take hold. I sat in the chair next to Dad, holding his hand, and eventually fell asleep.

I woke up around ten o'clock totally delirious and hungry. Dad's breathing was starting to slow and soften. He had been given morphine a couple of times since the breathing tube had come out because his breathing had become so labored and difficult. The nurse said he was probably in pain. I started getting agitated, and grabbed my phone, hoping to distract myself.

Suddenly I couldn't hear him breathing anymore. I looked up and watched Dad's face morph as his spirit left, as though it were climbing out of an uncomfortable piece of clothing. I leaned over and kissed him on the forehead.

"I love you Dad, you get to go home now. I'm so happy you get to see your father; he'll be waiting for you. I know how much you've missed him."

Dad's skin was on fire, I could feel his struggle to let go, to get out of his body.

What normally takes just a few minutes took Dad two-and-a-half hours. It was 10:23 p.m. I kissed him one final time, said goodbye, and took Mom home.

Walking into the house, it hit me, the full weight of knowing that Dad was gone. The house felt cavernously empty without his presence.

I know Mom felt it too. She stepped forward into the middle of the family room, looking around slowly. Her eyes moved around the room, looking at nothing.

"I don't want to stay here," she said. "I don't want to stay in this house."

I was so tired that every muscle and joint in my body ached, and I was filled with dread. Whatever was to unfold after this day, I knew it would not be good. I looked at my mother and sensed the oncoming shift in her stability like a wave gathering to begin its thunderous crash to the shore. I was exhausted, overwhelmed, and shattered by the emotional turbulence of the past few days. How was I ever going to get through what lay ahead? I gritted my teeth and shut my eyes against her relentless focus on herself. There was no sense of team work here. She had no empathy for what I was going through. I would manage. I had tools. Didn't I?

CHAPTER 8

ARRANGEMENTS

May 29, 2015

I woke up at eight. Mom was already clearing out closets and throwing things away. I was angry at first, as I wanted to go through Dad's things. But I knew it was her way of coping. I inhaled as slowly as I could.

"Can you not throw anything of Dad's personal items away?" I asked.

"Like what?"

"Like watches and things that Dad held dear. Where is Dad's wedding ring?"

"I don't know, I'm just getting rid of all his medical supplies." It was hard to breathe, and I felt dizzy. I couldn't watch Mom go through Dad's things so effortlessly, like she was taking out the trash.

"I have to go. I'm meeting Aunt Pat so we can go to Schrader's."

Schrader's is the funeral home on Main Street in downtown Plymouth that has been in operation for more than one hundred years. If you were born and raised in Plymouth, you had your service at Schrader's. Aunt Pat lived a few blocks away. There were so many decisions to be made, and I didn't want to make any of them, but Mom hated leaving the house and she would not have been an asset in the decision-making process. I felt numb inside and completely shut down.

I walked into Aunt Pat's house, crying.

"I don't know what to do. I'm so overwhelmed already."

"Well, first step is to go to the funeral home and get everything set up." Aunt Pat was very matter of fact. We were never a touchy-feely family. Very rarely was there hugging or kissing and although Aunt Pat showed no visible tears I could feel her sadness. Dad was her big brother, and she was his best friend. He shared things with her he never shared with Mom and me.

As we walked up the sidewalk, the front door of the funeral home opened and a middle-aged man in a suit greeted us. The place felt very comfortable inside—quiet, clean, and ornately decorated with red carpets. Eighteenth century art graced the walls and beautifully carved wooden end tables were scattered about. There was nothing disposable about the furnishings. We entered a small office.

"Hello, I'm George. I'll be helping you with all the arrangements."

George was a tall, thin man with white hair. I can't imagine how many times he had to go through this process, and he was seamless. Aunt Pat and I sat there as he asked a million questions. What type of service and service book? Did we want food and a priest? What type of casket? Where were we having him buried? Did we have the death certificate? Would we be writing the obituary for the Plymouth Observer and the Detroit Free Press? I was so relieved to have Aunt Pat with me. Even though I knew what Dad wanted, it felt strange to be making these decisions. Everything felt so final – the headstone and casket I chose would be forever on display, the permanent representation of Dad's life. How do you adequately honor a man's entire life in an obituary or a headstone? My mind went blank.

George took us upstairs to look at caskets. We entered a room filled with dozens of them, all different colors and materials. Dad had said he just wanted a pine box, nothing fancy. To my surprise there really was just a plain rectangular pine box, for $1,100. I laughed.

"Aunt Pat, there really is just a pine box! I can't in good conscience put Dad in that. It's horrible."

We both laughed and agreed. The next "cheap" model was also pine, but with a lovely stain finish and beautiful white satin lining with cushioned edges and a pillow for Dad's head. The handles were strong and made from pine and bronze. It was quite elegant and only three hundred dollars more, so we settled on that one. It was so surreal to be picking out a casket, it's akin to shopping for a sweater or pair of pants. You just pick out the one you like.

We went back downstairs and started talking finances. I had no access to Dad's bank accounts yet and didn't know how I was going to pay for any of this. Aunt Pat agreed to pay for everything, and I would pay her back when we got the life insurance money. I was blown away by the cost. We did everything as cheaply as possible, and we even got the headstone for free because Dad had been in the Air Force, but it still added up to nearly ten thousand dollars.

"What do you want the headstone to say?" George asked. I froze. I looked at Aunt Pat. I had no idea, I felt so stupid.

Aunt Pat broke the silence and said, "Beloved Father, Brother, Husband."

We wrapped things up and I watched as Aunt Pat graciously wrote George a check. I felt guilty that I was not prepared for this. I was not used to asking for help and I didn't like it.

This was a Friday, so we decided to have a simple service on Monday night for all of Dad's friends, with the burial on Tuesday just for family. We went back to Aunt Pat's house. Uncle Steve was there. I love the man, but he can be hard-headed and liked to scream a lot.

"Did you contact the attorney yet?" he asked, loud and impatient.

"No, I can't remember who they are."

Years ago, Dad had sent papers for me to sign so I could become his Medical Power of Attorney and Trustee. I signed them and filed my copy away in a box. At the moment, I had no idea where the box was. (I found it years later.) Luckily, Aunt Pat had a copy, and she gave me the attorney's name and number.

"Now, you're going to have to make a lot of decisions over the next few months."

"I know, Uncle." He was talking to me like I was a stupid, helpless woman, and for a moment I resented him. But then a small voice inside said, he doesn't really know what I'm capable of.

"You should drive over there today and get some answers about the accounts." I was sensing he was a little angry and irritated that Aunt Pat had just paid for all of Dad's burial expenses.

"I understand, Uncle. I'll see what I can do."

I drove off and headed towards Livonia. For some reason my GPS wasn't working right, and I kept getting lost. I'd been gone from this city for twenty years now and I'd forgotten where things were. After my third failed attempt to find Morello Law Group, I headed home. I found out later that Uncle Steve had given me the wrong address. I was so overwhelmed I didn't think to check it myself.

I pulled up in front of the house. Bags and bags were already piled high on the curb. Mom had been cleaning. I went inside and found her sitting on the sofa, staring off into space. I started to get concerned. I hadn't really seen her cry or mourn that much in any sense. She still had that empty look in her eyes. I decided I couldn't talk to her, much less look at her. It would send me back into the past, and I couldn't afford to go there right now.

CHAPTER 9

OLIVIA

When my home life in high school became more stressful due to my mother's undiagnosed mental illness and my father's denial around the desirability of doing anything about it, my best friend Olivia's family became my adopted family. Her mother, Sally, took me in as one of her own—she already had three kids—and gave me a place of safety and a sense of normality. Olivia and I met in ballet class when we were twelve, and we were also in the marching band color guard together in high school. I thought back then we could not be more opposite, but we understood who the other was and shared a deep bond.

It wasn't until I got sober that I realized how similar Liv and I actually were emotionally and how our connection had been forged. Our so-called differences turned out to be only superficial preferences. Olivia was living in Maumee, Ohio, by the time my father died, and she was divorced and raising two children on her own. Yet she drove almost an hour-and-a-half to see me in Plymouth, where her parents lived.

The drive from my parents' house in Redford to Plymouth is only twenty minutes, even at 5:15 p.m. on a Friday. I love that drive. When interstate I-94 changes into state road M14, the landscape shifts into a vernacular of green grass flanked with woods, hidden streams, and an occasional water tower peeking up over the treetops. It's easy on the eyes and creates an opening inside of me. Driving through it on the way to see Olivia, I was finally able to take some deep breaths with long exhalations.

When I was a child, many of the country roads, including the one I grew up on, were dirt. The road to Sally's house was still unpaved and I loved driving on it, potholes and all. They make you slow down. It feels like an entrance into nature's territory, a signal that I've officially left the city and the automated world of humans. Sally and her husband, Dr. Robert Welch, were in their car, coming out of the driveway when I arrived. We both stopped. Sally and I got out and embraced.

"I'm so sorry to hear about your father. We're going out to dinner, so you and Liv can have some space. She's inside," Sally said.

"Thanks," I replied. Continuing up the driveway is like a magical wonderland. Dr. Welch had built a sport fishing pond in the front yard, and stocked it with trout, bass, and bluegill. Willows and maples lined the lane, and I could just see, in my mind's eye, the incredible fall colors. It's as picturesque as an English country home—my ideal house.

I walked up the cobblestone path and rang the bell. Liv opened the door, I walked in, and we hugged. Tears that I had been holding back were able to come forth, up through my heart and lungs to find their expression, but only for an instant. They choked back on their own.

"You don't have to be so strong, you can let go. You can let go."

But I couldn't. I felt as rigid as stone.

We sat on a velvety couch in the large great room with tables on each end, heaped full of framed family photos. Something you'd never see in my parents' home.

"Thank you so much for driving up here to see me, I know it wasn't easy for you," I said. She had worked that day and had had to find someone to watch her kids at the last minute.

"I wouldn't miss being here for you." My independent self-reliant nature was getting tested on this trip. My dependency on Aunt Pat for her physical and financial support, and now Olivia's grace, were beginning to crack the walls around my inability to receive. "So, what happened?" Olivia asked.

"The doctors don't really know. They ran a battery of tests and didn't find anything wrong with Dad's heart. No sign of stroke or heart attack. They asked if I wanted to do an autopsy, but I said no."

We chatted a bit more and I could feel her examining me closely. This woman knew everything about me—could read me like a book.

"You can let go. You're the strongest person I know, but you don't have to be strong with me."

I could feel another sledgehammer hit the walls of my protection and the cracks continued to radiate. More tears started to flow, but they stopped themselves again. Something I couldn't identify would not let me go there.

"Mom, Dad, and I will be at the service," Olivia continued and then went on to offer to contact people from our high school. I just didn't have the energy for it.

We shifted the conversation to high school gossip to lighten the mood. We laughed at how some people didn't age as well as others and snickered at people's life choices. It was not the best use of time, but it helped me feel better about my own choices. Liv was much more involved in post-high-school activities than I was and regularly caught up on Facebook with what everyone was doing. When I moved to San Diego, one of my intentions had been to start over with a clean slate: this was a place where no one knew who I was or where I came from. I wanted to leave people, places, and things behind. I resented the small-town mindset of Plymouth; it was oppressive. There were so many unsubstantiated rumors and misperceptions about me that had formed people's idea of me. To most, I was a lost, fuck-up girl. I couldn't stand it. I would be shocked if anyone came to Dad's funeral.

Liv needed to get back home to her kids, so we said our goodbyes. "I'll see you Monday. And thanks again for coming up. I love you," I said.

"I love you, too. See you Monday."

Driving home, I was thinking about the weekend. Being the trustee to Dad's estate, I needed to go through his famous five-foot tall, four-drawer, black filing cabinet, which contained his whole life.

The year I was a junior in high school, Mom and Dad were fighting so much that Dad ended up moving to Aunt Pat's for a month and when he left, he took the filing cabinet with him because Mom loved to burn important documents in the fireplace when she thought no one was looking, although I saw her doing it countless times. Important things always seemed to go missing around my mother and still do. Whenever papers would disappear, Dad would ask Mom where they were and her typical response, delivered with an insulted twang in her voice, was "I don't know, I have no idea." So, Dad had to take precautions to keep her from destroying everything. I haven't the foggiest idea why he didn't simply lock his filing cabinet.

Dad had been buying rental properties long before he met Mom, believing that it would make him a millionaire. Even though Dad's properties were all held in his name only, the law in the state of Michigan says that he had to get spousal approval on any sale of a property or when he wanted to refinance one of them. A series of bad financial decisions left Dad needing to refinance some of his houses at several points during his life, so he was in a position of needing Mom's signature fairly regularly. But one of Mom's biggest triggers was being asked to sign things. It made her paranoid. For months, she would refuse to do as he asked.

One day, while I was still living at home, I was sitting in the kitchen eating lunch when Dad came in and said, "You have got to sign these papers, Susan."

"I'm not signing anything. I don't even know what they're for."

"You know exactly what they're for. Do you realize that if you don't sign these documents, we are not going to have any money to send Heather to college?" Mom stared at him.

"I don't care."

It was the last straw. Dad moved out a week later.

His action prompted one of Mom's rare moments of clarity about her condition. She'd known since high school that she wasn't right, mentally, but never had the resources to get help. This time, threatened with the possibility of losing Dad, she promised she would get help. Dad in his naiveté, moved back in. The filing cabinet was reinstated in his office. Mom didn't get help. Things returned to exactly how they had always been.

The cabinet contained every bill, bank account statement, insurance policy and any other important paper Dad had ever received, and I would now have to go through all of it. I had no time for grief. I told myself I had to stay focused and create a game plan of what needed to be done. And so that's what I did.

CHAPTER 10

VISITATION

May 31, 2015

On Sunday, I went to Aunt Pat's to look through pictures and create a photo board to have at the service. She had asked me earlier to bring some pictures from home. Much to my sadness, we didn't have a lot of photos of Dad past my early childhood. We were not a picture-taking family. Growing up, I always envied my friends who, year after year, had their family portrait done and proudly hung it on their wall. That was never us. Mom and I went through some boxes and picked out four photos. Dad in his air force uniform. He and I together when I was a baby, another when I was a toddler. And a picture of him and his mom with one of his drag racing cars. Grandma loved to cheer him on and ride with him. Dad was a momma's boy; he could never do wrong in her eyes. Even though I never met her—she died of cancer just two days before I was born—I have always felt very close to her: she left this Earth as I was coming in and as we passed each other in the portal she blessed me with her strength. To this day I envision her as a guardian angel keeping watch over me.

I showed up at Auntie's house with my four pictures, and we got to work upstairs in a little nook of her house just off Audra's old bedroom. We accessed it through a tiny door—imagine a door for a doll house, one like Alice from the "Wonderland" books might have used when she grew too large for the room she was in. The room itself was full of craft supplies, sewing materials, antiques, and all sorts of things that could be used to make floral arrangements. Aunt Pat a very gifted designer, opened Ribar Floral on Main Street in 1984 and retired decades later, but she still had the remnants of her success.

We sat down at a long card table and dumped four plastic shopping bags full of pictures from the last fifty years onto it.

"I know there are pictures of Ken in here somewhere," she said, laughing.

"This will be fun, going through our family's history."

Dad had never volunteered much about his family. He would answer my questions with only very short replies. Aunt Pat, on the other hand, was very willing and able to share with me what she knew about the Moore and Pustelek families. Dad and Aunt Pat had been the first in their family to go to college. Dad went to Devry Tech in Chicago and got an AA degree in electronics while Aunt Pat got a BA in English from Eastern Michigan. We spent hours going through photos and found dozens of pictures of Dad to display at the memorial. We hooted and hollered as Aunt Pat shared memories of their childhood. Dad liked to take things apart. One time, out on Uncle Leo's farm, he took apart some tools Uncle Leo had been using and buried the pieces out in the yard. Uncle Leo caught on to Dad's game and banned him from the barn.

After we finished, I went home to rest. The remainder of the weekend was spent on the couch, a short trip to the mall, watching TV and renting on-demand movies. I didn't want to think about anything. I needed to zone out and shut my brain down for a while.

*   *   *

June 1, 2015

I woke up on Monday to another beautiful sunny day. Dad's service was scheduled for four o'clock. I went to meet Aunt Pat at Schrader's for some final paperwork and to deliver Dad's burial clothes. It was a no brainer, what he would have wanted to go in the ground wearing: his favorite light blue Levi's, white Nike sneakers, a Michigan sweatshirt and a Michigan hat. He very rarely wore a non-Michigan shirt, and he always had his hat on.

I was relieved that Aunt Pat and Kelly had invited all our friends and family members, and Dad's co-workers, to the service. I was curious to see who would come: I saw Dad as a loner. I don't even know the last time he had been out with any friends. I thought it had been years, if not decades.

I moved slowly through the day, as if my life were suddenly on pause. Between shock and grief, I was going through the motions of living. My mind was trying desperately to find a sense of stability, but nothing was normal and never would be again. As the time to get ready approached, I had no idea what to wear. I definitely was not wearing black. Too morbid. I settled on jeans, a tank top and a dark blue cardigan sweater.

Mom didn't have anything to wear for the burial, so I had taken her to JCPenney over the weekend and we got her some new pants and a shirt. I could feel her discomfort, as though she didn't deserve to be wearing nice clothes. She looked nice in her new outfit, and I was relieved to see that she was *present*.

Once we got in the car, things changed. She began fading away. I looked in her eyes, but no one was there. We hadn't even hugged since Dad had passed, and I hadn't seen her cry since the hospital. I felt a pang of pity for her, while simultaneously feeling unwilling to be there for her.

As we approached Schrader's I could see Dad's school bus in the parking lot. A massive banner hung on the side saying "Ken, We Will Miss You!" Later I found out that each bus had flashed their red lights to honor Dad that morning as they left the bus yard for their runs. A memorable farewell. The gesture took my breath away. I felt so happy for Dad: he was honored by people who really cared about him. Tonight, we would get to celebrate his life.

Mom and I walked in to hear 1950s pop music playing, at Aunt Pat's request. Dad never listened to music; he was strictly an AM news radio and weather program kind of guy. I felt comforted by the sound of my family's laughter and appreciated seeing my cousins and second cousins look at the photographs that Aunt Pat and I had so meticulously chosen. To the right, at the front of the room, was Dad's casket, surrounded by beautiful wreaths of flowers that lit up the space—life joined with death. The room was quite large and had one small couch in the center facing the front of the room, with a coffee table and small chairs scattered throughout. There was red carpeting and wood paneling on the walls, old school Victorian. Mom immediately took a seat on the couch. People greeted her, but she didn't acknowledge them.

I said "hello" and hugged everyone, then sat down next to Mom and put my arm around her, even though I felt angry and uncomfortable in her presence. "How are you? Are you okay? Aren't you going to say 'hello' to everyone?" I had seen my mother talk to people in the past, although it wasn't her strong suit. She was certainly adept at hurling insults my way. And although it seemed as though she understood what had happened, she didn't seem to have any sense of what her role as The Widow might be in this whole social ritual. She looked around in a daze, her eyes moving in slow motion, her neck craning slowly, like an underwater sloth.

"I don't belong here. Do you want me to go, Heather?" she asked. I had never seen her this bad before. It was as though something else had taken over her, as though my real Mom was gone. She looked small and scared.

Fear shook through my body. She was completely gone. I felt the same sense of evil I had felt as a child, the familiar fear of the empty space where Mom was supposed to be, a space that yawned with vacancy. I lied.

"No, I don't want you to go. Don't you want to be here for Dad?" She got up and looked around, mumbling to herself.

"I don't belong here. I'm going to wait in the car for you."

"Mom, it's going to be hours before I leave. I'll have Kelly bring me home." I said.

"No, I'll wait for you in the car."

"Okay, see you later." I was relieved that she extricated herself, I wanted to crawl out of my skin.

I walked over to Dad's coffin and peered inside. It didn't look like him. His whole body looked swollen, his face was bloated, slightly disfigured, and he was cold to the touch. It was the oddest feeling staring down at him. *Is this really real? Dad is gone, but I'm staring at his body.* I didn't feel anything in that moment, cycling through feelings of shock and disbelief with a dash of numbness.

Suddenly a crowd started pouring in. Most of them were people from his work, dressed casually in jeans and orange reflective vests, some in orange T-shirts with Dad's name printed on the left side sleeve next to his bus number, 40A.

They'd managed to print 100 T-shirts in a couple of days in memory of my father. I started sobbing. The front of each T-shirt had a picture of a school bus full of kids with the tag line "*save a horse, ride a school bus!*" Laughter and joy filled the air as we all started talking about Dad. Every time someone new walked over and found him in his Michigan outfit they became giddy, and remarked,

"Oh, that is sooo Ken! How perfect. Could never imagine him in anything else." The procession formed a circle: come in, sign the book, walk over to dad, look at the picture board, meet Dad's sisters and my cousins, and then me. I was the last stop. Dozens of people said the same thing to me, over and over.

"Oh my gosh, you must be Heather! You look exactly like him." They told me how Dad talked about me all the time, always telling them how proud he was of me having my own business, and how much he loved me.

I wish Dad would have shared that with me; I felt shame, being the last one to know. People also mentioned repeatedly that he wished I had come home more and he thought I was too independent. Why was he so surprised? His mantra was *God helps those who helps themselves*. I was a product of the environment that he and Mom had created. I was doing my own laundry, getting myself to school and packing my own lunch by fourth grade. No one gently nuzzled me out of bed with kisses and hugs. I awoke to the ear-splitting sound of the alarm clock and curled my hair in the typical 1980s fashion: peacock bangs with Aqua Net hairspray. Sometimes I dressed like I'd walked out of a Victoria's Secret catalog, desperate for attention.

Everyone had their own personal story about Dad, how he had touched every single person in that room so deeply. His kindness and generosity toward others made even the most insignificant person feel important. Two stories affected me the most, one from a man who appeared to be in his late forties.

"Your father is the nicest person I've ever met. My first day on the job was scary. I was wondering, 'will I be accepted, what will the folks be like?' We have a break room where we all gather and I walked in for the first time, nervous as hell. Looking around, I just took a deep breath. From the other side of the room, your father walks over, stretches his hand out, looks me dead in the eyes and says 'Ken Moore, nice to meet you.' I will never forget that. He was just so incredible."

Yes, he was, I thought.

The second story was from the mother of one of the kids on Dad's bus for special needs kids. She came up to me in tears, sharing with me how much she loved Dad, and how her child had loved him, too. He had taken care of her baby in a way that no other driver had, and now this child was asking her, crying, "'Where is Mr. Moore?

"How do I tell my child he is gone?" she asked. "This is just too heartbreaking, such a wonderful man, his death has affected my family deeply."

My God, this poor woman. Her grief penetrated me. The level of trust and connection that she and her son must have felt with Dad were enviable and it's a demonstration of true human spirit which, sadly, is nearly lost in our culture. I felt as though I was learning more about Dad after his death than I'd known about him when he'd been alive.

Halfway through the visitation, I started feeling tired, hungry, and emotionally overwhelmed. Every one of the nearly 200 people who paraded before me had a hug, a story, a picture, and some tears. It was a lot to hold, and my face was starting to go numb from all the smiling and crying. Cousin Danny could tell I needed a break.

"You okay?" he asked. I snuggled into his football-player-sized chest and wrapped my arms around his waist.

"No, I need to go pee and be alone for a second."

"Go, I'll cover for you."

The click of the lock on the bathroom door let me know I was safe again. In my own space, I wanted to pound my fists against the wall and scream my head off, *This is so unfair, this sucks, Dad why did you leave me?!* I was stuck inside, and it would be hours until I could leave, to go back to a house that didn't feel like home, that was empty without Dad.

CHAPTER 11

THE FUNERAL

June 2, 2015

I woke up the next morning still numb. *We're burying Dad today.*

Mom and I drove out to Oakland Hills Cemetery. We were the last to arrive and everyone was waiting for us in their cars, having driven one by one through the cemetery to Dad's site. The flowers from the previous night were perched next to Dad's casket. I was surprised and happy to see two women from the Air Force there.

The day was warm, the sun was shining, and birds were singing joyfully. I wish I could have really felt the moments as they happened, but none of it seemed real. There was a man there to lead the conversation, but I don't remember what he said. The flag ceremony came next. The two women from the Air Force took the American flag from atop Dad's casket and started folding it meticulously.

Mom was standing next to me and grabbed my arm to make me come closer. It triggered a rage inside of me, ruining my ability to be present in the moment. I didn't want her touching me. Despite all the personal and spiritual development work I'd done I still felt a lot of anger and revulsion towards my mother. We're taught to let love lead the way and yet simmering inside me was a bitter question: "when had she ever shown me love?" I had borne the brunt of her hostile and condemning behavior for decades and I had forgiven her countless times. When was she going to express any kind or considerate sentiments toward *me*? She had embarrassed, humiliated, neglected, and judged me. My father was gone. And SHE wanted ME to support HER? I was pretty sure I hated her.

When the airmen had finished, the flag was a perfect, plump triangle. One uniformed woman walked over and presented it to me. It was beautiful and completely humbling.

Aunt Pat read the quote that was hanging next to Dad's hospital room:

> *Don't grieve for me, for now I'm free.*
> *I follow the plan God laid for me.*
> *I saw His face, I heard His call.*
> *I took His hand and left it all.*
> *I could not stay another day.*
> *To love, to laugh, to work or play;*
> *Tasks left undone, must stay that way.*
> *And if my parting has left a void,*
> *Then fill it with remembered joy.*
> *A friendship shared, a laugh, a kiss,*
> *Ah yes, these things, I too, shall miss.*
> *My life's been full, I've savored much,*
> *Good times, good friends, a loved one's touch*
> *Perhaps my time seemed all too brief—*
> *Don't shorten yours with undue grief.*
> *Be not burdened with tears of sorrow,*
> *Enjoy the sunshine of the morrow.*
> *—Anonymous*

"Goodbye dear brother, forever enjoy the hereafter, say hello to Mom and Dad," Aunt Pat said.

When she finished, the other airman played taps on the bugle as we walked over and laid roses on the casket. The morning was very peaceful, the air still and calm. The man officiating noted how unusual it was, at that time of year, to have a perfectly blue sky with no clouds or rain. And he pointed out how the birds had just kept singing. Dad loved birds.

We each walked over, put our hands on Dad's coffin, and said our final words. Mom kept reciting the Lord's prayer. It was obvious she wanted to contribute in some way, but that was all she could come up with. We were not there long, maybe forty-five minutes. I wanted to share something from my heart, something profound about Dad's life, but my mind was blank and my heart was broken. I felt that I'd missed the fullness and potency of the past two days. Going from one event to the next, emptiness filled my being. *Isn't there more I should feel?*

After we took turns scooping dirt into the grave, we headed off for lunch at Station 885 in Old Village, Plymouth. All twelve of us sat around two long tables joined together. Oddly, we didn't talk about Dad, or about what had just happened. The focus was on the plans we each had for the rest of the year.

Mom sat next to me at lunch. She seemed disturbed, staring off blankly into space.

"Do you want something to eat, Mom?" She switched her gaze to her plate but didn't respond. "Mom?" She continued to stare. I looked over at Uncle Steve, who tried to comfort her, rubbing her shoulders, but she didn't respond to him, either. *The lights are on, but nobody's home.* As I sat there floating in waves of childhood resentment, wishing she could be normal, I felt her loneliness and remembered that I still hadn't hugged her. I was still punishing her.

My mother's behavior started getting weird when I was about eight or so years old. She came from a very poor family in Mississippi, and she had no family or friends in Michigan, so I imagine she felt very unsupported after she married my dad. My dad—perhaps partly because he nearly nine years older than my mom, he was 31 and she 23—refused to include her in any decision making, which I'm sure she resented. For his part, my dad had had to give up his lifestyle and his dreams for his future once my mom came along. They argued constantly for a while and then my mom started doing strange things. She would come back from the grocery store, for example, and start asking me who was following her around putting strange food in her basket and asking her questions about her life.

"You *know* who's doing it," she would accuse me. What's more, I learned that there were certain topics—like Mom's family—that I had to avoid. If I ever asked her what it was like growing up, for example, she would angrily spit out, "it's none of your business," and ignore me for weeks. Sometimes she would stalk out on me, and I would have no idea what I'd done. Or my dad would do something to anger her, and she would go dark for three or four weeks. Eventually she would brighten back up like nothing had happened—she'd be happy cooking or doing some type of craft work and she'd be fine for a month or six weeks and then she would go off track again. I remember once when I was eight or nine years old my mother sat on the sofa in the living room in her pajamas for five months straight—doing nothing but stare out the window.

Things got to the point where my dad couldn't handle my mom, so he worked all the time and increased his interest in real estate investments. I only saw him about an hour a day, which meant I bore the brunt of my mother's bizarre behavior. By age eight I was making my own lunch and getting myself ready for school; my parents were nowhere to be found. I remember visiting a friend's house once and she climbed into her mother's lap to cuddle; I felt uncomfortable because my parents never hugged me or kissed me.

Dad became increasingly demanding as I grew up and I would only ever really hear from him was when I was doing something wrong. My grades were never high enough to please him and, ultimately, being home didn't feel safe. I was always on edge, feeling ready to fight or take flight: what's Mom going to say? What's Dad going to say? I knew something was wrong at home because I began to realize that other people didn't live that way. I was embarrassed and confused.

And dancing gave me refuge.

When I was three years old my mom put me in ballet classes and I kept dancing all the way through high school, where I was part of the marching band color guard. Dad bought me a car when I was sixteen, which meant I could be away from home as much as I wanted. I would spend most of my time at Olivia's house and her mom, Sally, gave me a semblance of normal family life my parents didn't. Sally also paid a month of college dorm fees when Dad couldn't pitch in.

By the time I was eighteen my dad had over-extended himself financially and he needed Mom's signature on paperwork relating to some investment properties he had to refinance. As usual, Mom wouldn't sign. He had been treating her badly for a long time by this point and she figured she wasn't obligated to make his life easier. So, Dad asked me to forge her signature; it wasn't too long after he filed for bankruptcy. My family situation was a mess and over the years I became adept at figuring things out on my own.

Through it all, my mom's odd and generally hostile behavior created a deep well of bitterness inside me that I could never shake. Why couldn't she behave reasonably? Why didn't she care about me? What was the matter with her? She wouldn't leave the house to see a doctor and Dad was in such denial that he refused to force the issue. We were one hugely dysfunctional family, and I became one hugely messed-up kid.

CHAPTER 12

AT THE LAWYER'S

June 3, 2015

The morning after the funeral, I loaded up the car with two suitcases of paperwork I had carefully selected from Dad's filing cabinet. I got to my appointment right on time. Wheeling all my baggage out of the elevator and into the office, the receptionist looked at me like I was nuts.

"Hello, I'm Heather and I have an appointment at eleven with George."

"George will be right in. Do you want coffee?"

"No thanks."

I had no idea that lawyers are worse than doctors when it comes to punctuality. I sat waiting for more than an hour in a big leather chair at a long table in a quiet conference room. *What if I had things to do? Are you supposed to take an entire day off to see your lawyer?*

Finally, George came in, accompanied by his paralegal, Stephanie. I disliked him immediately. He was in his mid-forties and had a medium build and dark hair, all of which was crowned by an incredibly arrogant and completely unsympathetic demeanor. He was not Dad's original counsel. Rob Johnson—who I had really liked—had worked with my dad to set me up as my dad's Medical Power of Attorney and get me appointed Trustee for his estate. I had spoken with him on the phone a couple of times, but he had left the firm to do his own thing.

We exchanged introductions and George apologized for being late. *Yeah, whatever.* I motioned to my suitcase and briefcase, and Stephanie immediately started going through everything. She was a well-dressed blond with very high heels and an assertive manner, and she began attacking my luggage with a robotic level of professionalism. I wasn't sure I liked her any more than I liked George.

"So, Heather," George said. He spoke slowly. "You are the trustee. However, I've gone through your father's trust and will and unfortunately the assets were never actually put into the trust."

I don't know what this means but it doesn't sound good.

"How can that be possible?"

"The trust is empty." My heart started pounding and I got a sinking feeling in my stomach.

"So, what does that mean?"

"It means that everything that was held in your father's name will go directly to your mother."

I froze. *This can't be right.* I was filled with rage and hurt. *Was this what Dad wanted? What was he thinking? Didn't he trust me? Didn't he think I could do it?*

"There has to be some mistake. There is no way in hell that my mother will be able to manage any of this."

"Your father shared with Rob your mother's condition so I am aware of the difficulties this will pose. Rob advised Ken many times to put all his assets in the estate. But apparently your father didn't do it."

Oh my God, oh my God, this can't be happening.

George continued talking but I couldn't hear anything he was saying. I was blowing up on the inside, literally a grenade just went off and my ears were ringing. I wanted to walk away. *What in the AF?* I felt panic rising like a flood; it was becoming hard to breathe. *What am I going to do?* What little I did catch was something about getting a conservatorship over my mother … "Probate court … very expensive."

Great.

It occurred to me that Mom would be the beneficiary on all their accounts. I wouldn't have access to any money. Mom wouldn't cooperate in the spending of a single dime, no matter how much she might benefit from it. She would resist all efforts to sort out her finances.

Towards the end of our two-hour conversation, most of which I spent wanting to run out of the room screaming, George said, "If you choose to work with us moving forward, I need you to sign a retainer. I charge $350 an hour and Stephanie is $175. The other option, instead of a conservatorship, is if your mom will sign over power of attorney to you. This would be the easiest option."

"Easiest option? My mother will never sign anything, she never has, and I'm sure she won't start now." I sighed. "But I'll ask her."

I scheduled a meeting at the lawyer's office for Mom and me for the next day. How I was going to get her there, I had no idea. I packed up my papers and drove home, sobbing uncontrollably. *Dad, why did you do this? Why didn't you take care of us? How am I going to pay for everything if I can't get access to the accounts? Don't you trust me? How am I going to deal with any of this?*

When I walked in the door, Mom was watching TV, looking somewhat comatose.

"How did the attorney go?" she asked.

"Not good, Mom. Dad didn't set the estate up right and now everything goes to you."

"But I thought you were the trustee?"

"I am, but Dad didn't put the assets into the trust, so I have no power. Would you be willing to sign a power of attorney? We have an appointment with George tomorrow. He wants to speak with you."

"Why do I have to go? You're the trustee."

Oh good God. Here we go. Talking in circles was Mom's M.O. Before you know it, you don't even know what you were talking about in the first place.

"Look it up on the computer Mom, I don't know what else to tell you."

Mom started to spin out. My worst nightmare. I felt like I was with Rain Man from that movie with Dustin Hoffman years ago, but I was with schizophrenic, unintentionally gas-lighting Rain Main.

I decided to run up to the Plymouth Community Federal Credit Union, to see if I could get something done there. I sat down with Paul, a young man in his twenties, and explained the situation.

"I'm sorry, ma'am, but Susan Moore is the beneficiary. I can't give you access to the account. Sounds like you will have to do a conservatorship or power of attorney."

"Yes, I realize that, but we have no access to money right now," I said.

"Bring your mother in here, we can give her access." *Agghhh. YOU DON'T UNDERSTAND! My mother is an undiagnosed paranoid schizophrenic. She will not come here and she sure as shit will not show you her driver's license.* I walked out fuming.

When I got home, I opened the car door and collapsed in the driveway with grief and rage. Mom came running out.

"What's wrong? Get in here, the neighbors are watching!"

Doubled over, I climbed the two stairs, entered the house, and fell on the couch, so hysterical I could barely breathe. Shock was wearing off, grief and helplessness were setting in, and the monster in front of me that was the estate and what to do with Mom was coming after me. Finally, I composed myself enough to be able to speak.

"We have to go to the bank. I cannot get access to the account."

"I have nothing to do with this. This is between you and your father. You are the trustee."

"Mom, you don't understand, how are you going to pay your bills? I am powerless. I can do nothing right now."

She continued to argue with me. I just wanted to die. I fell again, this time on the kitchen floor. I couldn't handle anything. Mom, seeing me bereft, had a fleeting moment of clarity and agreed to go to the bank.

"I'm driving," she said. Another thing we had been fighting about.

"How can you see? Fine." Mom has always been the worst driver, even when she could see. She sped through the neighborhoods. If the speed limit was 25, she went 40, never stopped at stop signs, and drove 50 on the highway, in the fast lane. Now she had cataracts and a pair of glasses that should have been retired in the last millennium.

When she wheeled Dad's Ford Explorer into the credit union parking lot she grabbed herself two parking spots. *Oh well. There's plenty of parking.*

"Hi Paul, this is my mom, Susan," I said when we got inside.

"Hi Susan, nice to meet you," Paul said, extending his hand.

"Oh, I have a cold," she said, refusing to shake. *Not true*, I thought. We sat down. Mom pressed her hands awkwardly over her purse, which she held against her stomach. Her elbows stuck out strangely.

"Okay Ms. Moore, can I see your driver's license?" Mom looked incredulous.

"What do you need that for?"

"To confirm your identity."

"For what?"

"To get access to your account."

"This isn't my account."

"I understand that, Mrs. Moore, but since your husband passed away, you are the beneficiary, and in order to give you access to the funds, I need to see your identification."

"This has nothing to do with me." She started manically smacking her lips, one of her tics that could always push me over the edge. It made her seem completely unhinged, like a wind-up toy, with the screw turned all the way, and then released. *Smack smack smack.* It drove me doubly mad because I have misophonia, which made me want to grab the letter opener and stab her in the eye.

"Mom, please, just show him your ID."

smack-smack-smack-smack

"This has nothing to do with me"

smack-smack-smack

"Heather is the trustee"

smack-smack

"She's crazy!" I screamed out, desperate to stop the awful sound, looking entreatingly at Paul. Mom just sat there, clutching her purse even more tightly, her elbows skewed out to the side, her face blank, her lips smacking away.

Paul motioned me into another room and shut the door.

"I can see that your mom is not well."

"Really?" Sarcasm oozed from my voice, through my tears. "That's what I told you."

"I'm sorry, but without a legal document, I can't help you."

"Fine. I'll be in touch." I walked Mom back out to the car, in a murderous rage. "Why did we come here, Mom?"

"I don't know, you said you needed to come."

"I explained to you at home what needed to happen and again you are defiant and selfish," I yelled. "If we don't do anything you are going to be homeless. I don't know why you have to make everything so fucking difficult."

"You are the trustee, Heather. This has nothing to do with me," she said again, in an accusatory tone that made me want to scale the walls. As she drove us home, I sat there in ruins, knowing that things were going to get a whole lot worse.

CHAPTER 13

CROSSROADS

I went to Aunt Pat's house a couple of hours later. I walked in, tears in my eyes. Everybody was there for family dinner. My body relaxed in the comfort, care, and company of my family. I loved my aunt and uncle's house. It was more than 100 years old, and my aunt was an antique country barn person so everywhere you go in her house you feel like you're in a country store. There was an original woodstove in the kitchen and an original red barn on the property outside. My aunt is super creative, and you feel the care and love and attention that goes into everything she does. Walking into that house has always been like coming home.

"So how did it go with the lawyer?" Aunt Mary asked.

"Not good. Dad didn't put the assets into the estate, so everything went to Mom."

Everyone in the room let out a simultaneous gasp of disbelief and in unison exploded with statements of incredulity.

"You're kidding me? No way! What? What was Kenneth thinking?"

"Your guess is as good as mine," I replied.

I don't know what the tone was before I walked in, but small heated conversations broke out around Dad and

Mom's relationship, particularly Dad's denial of Mom's mental state.

Everyone but Dad knew that something was wrong with Mom. Around my pre-teen years she had stopped leaving the house but before then she had attended community college and had had a somewhat normal life. Her journey off the rails began with the paranoid conviction that Dad and I were having her followed. A few years later, Mom became convinced that Aunt Pat was in on it too. Aunt Pat understood immediately what was going on.

"Your father came to visit me at work one day. 'Pat,' he said, 'I'm really sorry to ask you this, but … are you having Sue followed?' I was like, 'What? I'm working thirteen hours a day, seven days a week in my flower shop, when the hell would I have time to follow your wife around?' 'Well, Sue thinks you're having her followed.' 'Ken,' I told him, 'Your wife is schizophrenic.'" Two of Aunt Pat's husband's family members had schizophrenia, so she was familiar with the behavior. But Dad was in denial. Maybe he was embarrassed or maybe it was easier for him to say Mom was "difficult" than that she had a serious problem. Maybe he felt helpless and didn't know what to do. But what he *did* do was bury his head in the sand and pretend everything was hunky-dory between them. Needless to say, my parents' marriage was pretty horrible up until I was about twenty-five when there was a shift. But before then, neither one of my parents was getting their needs met and neither was listening to the other.

Eventually, Aunt Pat told us all to talk about something else. We grabbed our dinner plates and, there were a few moments of silence before any of us could come up with another topic. I felt horrible for creating so much tension and concern.

In small ways, my parents' relationship affected the entire family. It was a missed opportunity to have a sister-in-law, an aunt, a friend, to be vulnerable, to share the truth, to feel full-on joy at family events and gather with a united front when tragedy strikes. We are all connected to each other whether we are aware of it or not, and nowhere is this more apparent than within our family, which also highlights the importance of our ancestral lines. It's becoming more accepted in psychology-related fields to believe that our consciousness and unresolved trauma and emotional patterns don't die with us. Someone down the line will have to resolve it all, whether it's a family member or the state.

In my case, I had inherited the fallout from all of my father's denial of Mom's mental and physical health. She couldn't even see, for crying out loud! Apparently, he had once mentioned to a co-worker, Meredith—who became his good friend and confidant—that "all his ducks were in a row." If Mom were capable, this would be true, but this could not have been further from reality. How could an entire family see the truth that Dad had been so blind to for forty years? I realized, with a sinking heart, that the bottom line is that we all live in our own realities. Filters that are created through programing, conditioning and genetics. People believe what they want or maybe what they can handle. Denial is the most powerful drug I know of.

I began to reflect on that in my own life. How was I lying to myself? What truth was I obscuring? It undoubtedly had something to do with relationships with men.

By the time we finished dinner, we were laughing in the typical Moore/Ribar fashion and for a few minutes, my mind was free of concern or worry. The conversation shifted to my cousin, Audra, and her very lax parenting style. She was struggling emotionally after losing her husband the year before and trying to keep up the construction business he had left behind. Her lawyers hadn't been very helpful, and she had made many costly financial decisions. The tone of communication in our family, while always very sarcastic, was truly filled with love. I was relieved I was not the center of attention. It made me insecure, and I was no stranger to shame. I was afraid of judgement and never wanted to appear foolish or as though I didn't know what I was doing.

I helped with the dishes and said my goodbyes. Driving home, the pit in my stomach, which had disappeared briefly during dinner, returned. Tomorrow would be a crossroads. If Mom signed the power of attorney, we could move on easily. If not, we'd face a treacherous road ahead. When I got home, Mom was already in bed, and I followed suit.

The next morning, I woke up full of anxiety. I hadn't slept well now for days, and I could not get my body to relax. I was a ball of tension, my shoulders up to my ears, and my breathing shallow. At any moment I felt I could hyperventilate. I tried to talk to God and say some prayers, but I couldn't. Fear had completely taken over every part of my being, and I became stuck in a hyper-vigilant state that would last for months.

With the stress of Dad's death and its aftermath, all my years of knowledge of and experience with meditation as a way to stay centered, connected, and grounded became eclipsed by the responsibility of the estate and my inability to really grieve my father's death. Failing the ultimate test of my study, highlighting all the fragmented and traumatized areas of myself, I had yet to transcend my humanness. As I closed my eyes and tried to connect inside, I hit a brick wall. My heart said *hell no you're not getting in here.*

This surprised me. After studying sciences at Western Michigan University, I had gone to San Diego where I began working towards a master's degree in Chinese Medicine at the Pacific College of Health and Human Services. I had always been deeply intuitive, and very tuned in to nature, but I didn't look at my acupuncture studies as a spiritual pursuit. Chinese medicine is based on the Tao—the *natural* way of the universe—and this made sense to me. I had spent my childhood outside as much as possible looking for and finding safe places to just be me. As a little girl I was always running around the back yard or riding my bike, and there was a big maple tree in our yard against which I would lean sometimes, just to take in the peace it provided. In winter I would build igloos, and I would spend hours inside them just hanging out. At the back of our property was a low point where water would collect and when it froze, I would have an ice rink. We had a swimming pool in our backyard, as well, and what all of this meant was that I could be outside in all seasons. When I started studying Chinese medicine the conversation around the elements—water, fire, air, and earth—all made sense to me because I had spent so much time in nature.

Once I moved to California, I found another layer of "naturalness" through the people I met: they were more likely to be loving and kind than people had been in Michigan, and I discovered I didn't have to be quite so defensive. Everyone in California seemed to be searching for something—people knew they were probably messed up, but it was okay, and they talked about it. This was good for my heart and soul. I began to breathe freely for the first time in my life.

My mom had no religious convictions while I was growing up, but my dad had been raised a Catholic and apparently, he had wanted me to be raised as a Catholic, too. After I was baptized, though, he never mentioned anything ever again about me going to either a Catholic school or Catholic church services and so I wasn't exposed to a lot of religious indoctrination.

When I was twenty-four I read *Autobiography of a Yogi* and received a transmission, or what could also be called a "spiritual seeker initiation" from this book. I found out later that this experience wasn't uncommon, as it holds powerful energy for one who can receive it. After reading it, I got involved with the Self-Realization Fellowship, founded by the author Yogi Paramahansa Yogananda, who had come to the United States from India in the 1920s to spread yoga to the West—in fact for three years I lived across the street from a huge temple devoted to his teachings in Encinitas. I began meditating there and after two years of study I was initiated into Kriya Yoga. This is a very specific type of meditation meant to bring one into a state of Samadhi—the liberation from self-identification. I started drinking a couple of years later and these practices fell by the wayside. Almost ten years later and nearing the height of my drinking before I hit bottom, a friend invited me to a yoga studio in San Francisco to receive something called deeksha. I'll try just about anything to get out of emotional pain, so I accepted. Deeksha is a transfer of energy usually from guru to disciple and it's practiced throughout India. However, this gathering had regular people (meaning they were not gurus) giving the transmission. They were initiated and trained by Sri Bhagavan founder of Oneness University in Andhra Pradesh, India. I felt very calm receiving deeksha and started going regularly to the community's gatherings around the Bay Area. The purpose of deeksha was to alleviate one's identification with the mind, so you can move into deeper states of consciousness and witnessing, meaning less suffering. A few years later I went to Oneness University to escape a very abusive relationship and try and put the semblance of a life back together. I meditated for thirty days in a temple called Ekam. The building's sole purpose was enlightenment and just walking through the doors put visitors into higher states of consciousness, thanks to a variety of architectural enhancements related to sacred geometry and other energetic alignments. This center also provided training to people who wanted to become Oneness teachers.

A lot of what I learned at that time emphasized the idea that people tend to get stuck in their heads but if we get good enough at detaching from our mind, and our mind opens and flowers, then we can live more in our spiritual centers. I became steeped in the world of getting beyond the suffering we create in our minds and took many courses. I spent hours meditating and my friends at the time were all likewise training themselves to get beyond the suffering we create for ourselves through our thoughts and expectations. Some of this was relatively simple and some of the philosophy was more complex.

It was around this time as well that I began investigating ideas around parenting and ancestral patterns. Bhagavan taught that we are deeply programmed by our parents, and, in fact, everything that was happening between our parents and to them, from the time of our conception up until our birth, and for many years thereafter, has a huge impact on us. Were your parents fighting? Were they happy? Did your mother feel safe? All of this will have had an impact on you; it imprints us. The goal is to reprogram ourselves so that we are no longer at the mercy of the imprint. What makes the situation more complex is that any unresolved trauma people experience but don't resolve will be karmically seeded into the DNA of the next generation. I devoted a great deal of time and attention to clearing my own ancestral patterns and clearing programs passed on to me from both of my parents as well as my ancestors. I found ways to be centered and grounded. But in the wake of my father's death, with responsibility for my father's estate and my mother's care now firmly resting with me, I could feel myself losing my grip on my emotional stability. My spiritual training could barely get me through a conversation with my mother let alone see me through to the settling of my father's estate.

The day after my uplifting meal with my dad's side of the family, Mom came at me with all the "research" she had done on the internet regarding powers of attorney. Despite her erratic emotional behavior, she was wicked smart and the most creative person I knew. She could convince you to change your mind on just about any topic. Even if you were one hundred percent behind something to begin with, after listening to her, you could be questioning your beliefs.

"It says here I can do the power of attorney myself; we don't need to go through the lawyers."

"Okay," I said. "Are you going to do that?"

"It also says that the trustee can trump anything that the power of attorney can do."

"Whether or not that's true, you still aren't listening to me. I was yelling again. "This is assuming the assets are in the estate, which they are not. How many times do I have to say this?"

Mom is also the most stubborn person I know. Once she gets an idea in her head you cannot get her to budge. Heels ... are ... dug ... in. As a child I had carefully learned to tip-toe around certain loaded topics and I would choose my words precisely to avoid putting ideas in my mother's head about what I was doing or wanted to do. But the downside of this was that I also learned that my thoughts and feelings were not important or valued. Unfortunately, as I was to later learn, this is the beginning of the imprinting of addictive behavior.

"We need to eat breakfast and get ready to go," I said. "It won't hurt you to at least talk to George. If you won't listen to me, maybe he can talk some sense into you."

I knew that was probably a long shot, but I had some hope left. A hope that God would bless me and make this a little easier.

"Okay, I'll go. But I'm not changing my mind," she said. It was that tone again, the one that made me want to gouge her eyes out. So full of condescension, so full of the sure belief that she knew better than me, so full of absolute control over me. That tone said, "*I RULE!*"

Back in the conference room where I had waited for George for more than an hour the day before, the receptionist brought us coffee. All I could do was stare off into space. Mom tried to make small talk with me, but I could not look at her. Finally, George came in with Stephanie, sat down across the large oak conference table, and introduced himself and Stephanie.

"So, as Heather probably told you," he said to Mom, "the assets of Ken's estate are not in the Trust. Are you able to handle paying the bills and selling the houses?"

"This has nothing to do with me. Heather is the trustee. I don't understand why I'm being asked to sign documents."

He went on the explain to Mom what I had already spent hours beating my head against the wall to get her to believe.

"You're correct. Heather is the trustee of the estate. But for reasons we don't know, Ken did not transfer the assets into the trust. He did not sign the paperwork that would do that. So therefore, everything defaults to you, Mrs. Moore, because you are the beneficiary and his spouse. Heather currently does not have any authority to access any bank account or sell any of the houses. If you would just sign this paperwork, it will give Heather that authority."

"Well, I just don't believe that," Mom said, her arms folded firmly. "It states in the will that Heather is the trustee and will take care of the estate, so this has nothing to do with me. I'm not signing anything. I'm not signing away all my legal rights. She could have me committed." She pushed the paper towards him and looked away.

For just a moment I thought it was interesting that she focused on the possibility, *that I would have her committed.* Then I wondered if she was doing this on purpose. Throughout my entire life I had always felt like Mom had it in for me. It felt like every step I took to be successful or joyful would trigger her to try to pull me energetically back into her web of chaos and craziness. For example, I knew for a long time that I wanted to move to San Diego, so six months before my friends and I were due to move we decided to fly out there and find a place to live. There was no internet in 1995, so your actual plane tickets were delivered in the mail. For weeks I'd been asking Mom if she had seen my tickets and she said "no" nearly a dozen times.

A few days before we were supposed to fly out, I still hadn't received my ticket. Frantically, I called Northwest Airlines. They told me my ticket had been delivered weeks earlier and the confirmation receipt had been signed by a Susan Moore. When I confronted my mom with this information she decided to tell me that, yes, she had signed for a ticket, but it had been to Atlanta. I called Northwest back and they overnighted a second ticket to a friend's house. Stuff like this happened all the time. For my own sanity, it was best if I didn't engage.

We left the lawyer's office. I was angry, resentful, and hurt, reeling in complete frustration. *Jesus Christ, could this get any fucking worse?* My head was pounding. I just wanted to go back to my house among the redwoods of Marin County where I now lived. I longed for my friends, my bed, and my belongings; I desperately needed comfort. I would be heading home soon, but not soon enough.

As the afternoon ended, I went over to my cousin Kelly's for our last farewell. I loved spending time with her and her family—they could always find comic relief in the greatest of disasters. After pizza and a fulfilling conversation, Kelly walked me out to my car.

"So, what are you going to do?" she asked.

"I'm done. I don't want to help her. She can be homeless for all I care. I haven't even grieved Dad yet. I need to go home to peace and quiet. But as of right now, I'm walking away."

Kelly was shocked by my reply but didn't want to tell me what to do. We'd both been raised to believe that family members help each other, that we don't abandon one another, no matter what. But the people who had invented that mantra didn't have a father who abdicated his responsibility for his mentally ill wife. They hadn't met my mother. What's more, I hadn't asked to be in this situation. My mother was impossible to deal with, and this catastrophe was shaping up to be much harder than I felt I could possibly handle. Kelly simply hugged me and said "I love you. I know you'll do the right thing."

The sunset was gorgeous; it was a perfect June evening. Back in Redford, I sat outside on the stoop and lit a cigarette, watching the fireflies display their rituals. I wished I could be one, even just for a moment. I took a few deep breaths, relieved to be leaving in the morning. I wanted my life back: no drama, no crazy, a simple peaceful routine, free from stress and worry. I had worked hard for years to be able to live in peace. I was fulfilled. And now this.

CHAPTER 14

THE ESTATE

June 5, 2015

It felt good to be back in California. I walked out the baggage claim doors at San Francisco International Airport and caught the Marin Airporter to San Rafael, where my friend Georgia would be picking me up. I took in a deep breath and allowed the salty, foggy air of the Bay to calm my nerves as I began to settle into myself. I was looking forward to going back to work and focusing on something other than death and weirdness.

The familiar landscape was deeply relaxing. I knew what to expect at every turn. No surprises. After traffic on Route 101 and 19th Avenue, the shuttle bus crossed the Golden Gate Bridge and climbed into the Marin headlands where I began floating in a sea of calm. My breathing normalized, and for the first time in ten days I felt like I could cope. My head started to clear. Georgia picked me up, a kindness I very much appreciated and I felt the warm embrace of friends and my own home, the people and places I had *chosen* for myself, rather than been thrust into relationship with.

I lived in a beautiful rural community in a stunning redwood forest, and my tiny 300-square-foot house was built on stilts clinging to the side of a steep hill. There were beautiful redwood trees sitting at three points of the house itself and I had a large wrap-around deck that meant I could go out and sit in the warm embrace of these gorgeous trees any time I wanted. Some redwood trees grow to more than 300 feet tall and some have been known to have had a lifespan of up to 2,000 years. These trees symbolize strength, longevity, and power. It was heavenly to be home!

When I stepped into my tree house I fell onto the bed and stared out the window at the trees that helped prop up my little cottage. I lived in a redwood forest, a half mile from Samuel P. Taylor Park. My surroundings were replete with birds, deer, bobcats, and coyotes. I felt incredible calm and peace. For about ten minutes. Then my mind started to kick in. *I need to call Patricia and discuss what I should do.* I had met my mentor and friend Patricia, a woman of great wisdom and insight in her early seventies, through Oneness University. She led the women's meditation group I'd been attending for many years.

As I lay on my bed trying to focus on my breathing, I was simultaneously counting down the minutes until I could go see her. I was trying desperately to stay grounded and detach from the hypervigilant state that was a recognizable echo from my childhood. I felt like I had taken a beating every day in Michigan and I needed space and stillness before I could come back into myself.

I stared at a picture of Dad—my favorite one—that I had brought back from this trip. He was around my age in this picture—probably thirty-nine or forty—and although he's the only person in the frame his face had just erupted into joyful laughter as he listened to something the person sitting next to him at a neighbor's annual Christmas Eve party was saying to him. The photographer had managed to catch a moment in time when Dad was in his true essence. There was a sparkle in his eye and a genuine happiness showing through that I hadn't seen in decades—he was probably sitting next to an attractive woman; he was friendly, warm, and playful.

"Dad, I love you. I'm so grateful we got to have time last summer together. I miss you." I talked to the photograph, touching it, and hoping that he could feel me. I became lost in loving memories of him.

Hours later, when I arrived at Patricia's house, I walked into open arms and the best warm hug ever.

"Tell me everything," she said. We snuggled up on the sofa, and I did a play-by-play of the previous week. Then I started sharing about the estate.

"I don't know what to do. I'm so angry and full of rage towards Mom, she seems to delight in making everything hard. I don't want to do this; I don't want to help her."

"What will happen if you don't help her?"

"Bills won't get paid, the four houses will go into foreclosure, and she'll be homeless."

Patricia looked at me with grave concern and a little shock. There was a long pause.

"*Can* you help her?" That question took me by surprise, and I felt a jolt run down my spine. I let out a long exhalation.

"Yes, I can help her. But it would take everything I have."

"You know, Sri Bhagavan (Founder of Oneness University) talks about how if we can help someone and we don't, we get massive negative karma."

Are you kidding me, dear God. That's all she had to say. That word… *karma.* I had spent the previous three years excavating ancestral patterns and generational trauma, i.e. karma, as well as my own childhood trauma and imprinting. Their dense heaviness was the straight jacket I had been in for most of my life until I started intentionally looking at these issues. I started to cry. Patricia brought me in close and held me.

"I know you didn't really have a mother. I'll be your mom through this. Whatever you need."

I appreciated her words and had a moment of feeling not quite so alone, but deep inside I knew that this was my journey, and that there wasn't much anyone could do to mitigate the impact of what I had to do.

"Do you want to go into the mediation room?"

"Sure."

I went in and knelt before the alter to my teacher, Bhagavan, and wept. I went deep into my heart and into an abyss of grief so deep I thought I was being swallowed alive. It sucked me in, and I let it. Staying with the experience, I could access the heaviness in my chest and the knot in my stomach. No thoughts, just pure emotion. I could feel that something within me was dying. I didn't want to go into my mind; I simply wanted to feel. After a few minutes, I felt a lightness in my body, a shifting of energy. Internally, I acknowledged the shift.

Take me my Higher Self, take me into this grief and the journey ahead. Give me strength and wisdom to do what is before me. Light my path so I don't stumble in the dark and fall too hard. Help me to liberate generational patterns and my own trauma. I can sense the magnitude of the situation, and I can't do this without you.

Peace and calm flowed into my body. I felt an inpouring of nourishment and rest; I needed to gather all my internal resources. I was taking a first step on the path of real spiritual and emotional maturity. I had a sense that the person I knew myself to be would die a little every day until the person I was meant to be would emerge, however long that took, but it was a beginning.

When I felt that the transmission from the Universal Intelligence (UI) I was complete, I lay down to integrate. Anxiety started to creep back in, but I would try to take this situation one day at a time, from this moment forward. I was ready.

I went into the living room and hugged Patricia.

"Thank you for helping me *not* make a huge mistake."

"I'm so proud of you."

I called my attorney, George Fekaris, the next day and told him I wanted to move forward with the conservatorship.

"That's fine, but because I've already spoken to your mom about the power of attorney and she refused, having me do the conservatorship is a conflict of interest. I need to refer you to another attorney. The one I've picked out is a good attorney. Our firm will continue working on the estate side."

Great. So now I have two attorneys. This will cost a small fortune.

The weight of generational trauma can be an invisible burden. I knew the path ahead would be strewn with obstacles and difficulties. Dense ancestral energy had been passed from my parents' family lineages onto me, bringing an operating system marked by depression, mistrust, poor relationships, poverty consciousness, and disconnection. It moved through our family line like faint shadows in the wind. This ancestral energy had influenced my parents' identity, behavior, and perception without their knowledge or consent.

Most people face challenges where no matter what they do, the same pattern keeps repeating. There's no clear origin point— it's just the way things have always been. It's generational. Families contain a puzzling amount of "unfinished business," and unfortunately, subsequent generations are often less equipped to cope than those who passed down these patterns.

Murray Bowen developed Family Systems Therapy specifically to help people understand and heal this unresolved pain and the field of epigenetics recognizes that trauma can trigger physiological changes that predispose people to chronic illness; these changes can be passed to the next generation. This manifests as worsening emotional regulation, identity issues and a reduced ability to adapt to stress and chronic disease.

So, imagine that the thoughts, beliefs, and attitudes you're operating from aren't even yours. They come from three, four, or eight of your ancestors. If you come from a happy family, congratulations—you are very blessed. But most of us come from families marked by continued dysfunction or loss.

Our parents, grandparents, great-grandparents, or ancestors beyond may have carried strong poverty consciousness or chronic anxiety. They may have been prone to shame, low self-worth, or perfectionism. Perhaps they were easily angered or held onto grief. These tendencies transmit through generations via behavioral, psychological, or neurochemical patterns—even to those who have never experienced the original triggering events.

The challenge is that this generational imprinting happens entirely below conscious awareness. To create a happy, fruitful life, we must transform these patterns so we can lead a purposeful and fulfilling life. The key to this transformation is awareness.

When all Dad's wealth defaulted to my mother—who couldn't even write a check let alone manage an investment portfolio—it became a head-on reflection of his inherited web—denial, entrapment, pain, and living from duty rather than joy.

It also triggered my feelings of childhood abandonment and all the other issues that went along with it. Not being seen, heard, or mirrored, feeling abandoned, neglected, and ignored (which was exactly how my mother felt growing up and, from an outsider's perspective, how she seemed to feel being married to my father). This created an edge in me between impulsive and acceptable behavior, paving the way for my addictions, my predilection for reckless actions. My general attitude was *how far can I push myself before total annihilation?*

The biggest ancestral belief that blocked me in the ten months following my father's death was: "Life is hard, and no one is there to help you." Dad said this often—perhaps from Catholic guilt—and I carried the belief that life is a constant struggle.

Piece by piece, I faced each emotion, each situation, each thread of binding so my mother and I could finally move forward. We were both stuck. I knew she was, though it would take me a couple of years to realize how stuck I really was, as well. This was all tied up with my tendency to give my power away to others who I thought knew better than me.

In order for me to have a mental grasp on all my estate responsibilities, I had to compartmentalize the different categories of to-dos. How was I going to pay for two attorneys, four mortgages, Dad's Explorer, the insurance policies, et cetera? Until the conservatorship was finalized by the court, which would take weeks, I couldn't pay for anything. There was a small insurance policy from Plymouth Schools, Dad's bus driving employer, but that would barely get us through a month of expenses. I had filled out the form by forging Mom's signature and faxing it back when I was still in Michigan. I didn't have the bandwidth to ask Mom to sign anything more.

I had called Ford Pension and the subsidiary, MetLife Life Insurance Company, when I was still in Michigan, and managed to get Mom in a coherent five-minute window: when the customer service woman asked if she could speak with Mom, she had agreed, which ultimately gave me access to all of Dad's Ford Pension benefits and allowed me to be able to call the company on my mother's behalf. The first miracle. The policy was worth $12,500, and was to arrive in a couple of weeks, along with Mom's pension payments. By the time all the money came in, we were already two months behind. As Dad had passed in May, many of the May expenses hadn't been paid. I was in sticker shock.

I organized and made stacks of bills and other types of paperwork which were to live on my kitchen table for the next few months: mortgages, bank accounts, utilities, insurance policies, social security, IRAs, his NRA membership, and other subscriptions. You really learn a lot about a person by how they manage their money. I couldn't believe how complicated Dad made his accounting. I am very simple: one bank account, one savings account, one IRA. Dad had four checking accounts at four different banks, two IRAs with two different managing companies, and four mortgages, each with its own lender. *Jesus Christ Dad, could you make this any more difficult?* The only reason I could think of as to why Dad did it that way was so that, if one bank went down, maybe the others would stay afloat.

It was very strange for me to be looking at all of this. Dad had been so private about his finances. It was like I was reading his diary with thoughts intended only for his eyes, and I felt very uncomfortable. Was this even any of my business? After all, Dad had left this for Mom to take care of.

The insurance checks from the bus yard and Ford came, surprisingly, within the week, and got deposited into a joint account I had opened at my bank for Mom and me. I had also completed a change-of-address form in Michigan so Dad's mail would be forwarded to me.

I knew the banks wouldn't help me until I had the conservatorship paper, so I started calling everyone else: utilities, home and auto insurance, credit cards, mortgages. I thought this would be easy, but I was sorely mistaken. First, I would call with my usual opener,

"Hi, my name is Heather Moore, and my father is Kenneth Moore, he passed away on May 28. I need to update the mailing address and make a payment on his account."

"Oh, I'm so sorry for your loss. Can you mail an original death certificate, and then fill out some documents I will send you in an email?"

Out of the dozens of people I spoke with over the weeks, only two or three expressed sincere sadness that my father had died. It was the same thing every time, as though they were reading a script. The triteness, the insincerity, seemed to take something away from me and my grief. *I'd rather they not say anything at all.*

Secondly, anything I expected would involve a simple phone call to resolve an issue, took weeks, sometimes months, to get resolved. I was baffled and often suffered fits of rage when I couldn't get the documents I needed and had to call back.

"I don't know who you talked to but that isn't the correct information. And I also can't see a record that you called. There is no documentation." I kept impeccable records, so I could cite back to them the day, time, and person I had spoken to, and yet this happened at least twice with every single bank and lender. I couldn't believe it. *Do any of these people know what the fuck they are doing?* I wondered. Citizen's Bank held $250 dollars hostage for more than a year and they were horribly rude. They kept wanting a power of attorney from Mom, which I told them repeatedly they were never going to get but that a conservatorship document gave me legal rights to that money. The only financial institution that knew exactly what they were doing was Charles Schwab. I cannot recommend them highly enough. Their staff members were incredibly helpful and on the ball.

The administrative setbacks would send me into raging fits of hellfire. Countless times I would get off the phone, jump on my bed, and start screaming and beating into my pillows. "I fucking hate this! I HATE THIS! FUCK YOU, DAD, FUCK YOU, MOM, I NEED SOME GOD DAMNED HELP!"

I was letting the web consume me. The more I struggled, the more tangled in it I became. My fighting nature wanted to beat the situation into submission; into the gutter until the bitter end. But the lesson I had to learn was not about fighting, but about letting go and trusting, and I had no real idea how to do either.

MOM'S BROTHERS

Mom's brothers, Ron and Edwin Perry, live in northern Mississippi where they grew up. Uncle Ed lives in their hometown of Oxford and Uncle Ron lives in Tupelo about forty minutes east. In 1980—when I was five years old—Uncle Ron and his girlfriend had come for Christmas. They had brought a huge husky that Dad was not a fan of—it shed everywhere. They were told they could only come back if they didn't bring the dog. That was the last time I saw Uncle Ron.

There was very sparse communication over the years. Their daddy, Papaw as I called him, died in the summer of 1995, leaving a little bit of money to every one of his offspring and their kids, including me. Uncle Ed had given me my inheritance when Papaw died, but I knew Mom had never claimed hers. At the time, she had said to Uncle Ed that "Daddy didn't have any money. You're lying." So nearly $50,000 sat in a bank account for almost twenty years. I needed to buy a car and also wanted to do a month-long meditation retreat in India so I finally asked Mom in 2013 if she would gift me her inheritance and she said, "I told Ed years ago you could have it." So, I called Uncle Ed. I hadn't talked to him in a decade, but he was relieved to hear from me, stating that he had been thinking about calling me to give me the money. "I'm not going to be here forever, and I don't want to die with this money sitting here in the bank," he said. "Why don't you come down here and we can have a visit." I flew down to stay with him for a week and we had a cheerful reconnection more than thirty years after we'd first met. Now it was time for another, more difficult, conversation.

"Hello," he said, in his loud, southern way.

"Uncle Ed, it's Heather. I'm calling because Dad died."

"Oh Lord, I'm so sorry. How are you?"

"Not very good. Mom is by herself now in Michigan. I need to figure out what to do with her. Can you call her every so often?"

"Heather, the last time I spoke to your mother was over thirty years ago. She won't return my phone calls. I call her every year on her birthday, and I never hear from her." The anger in his voice made me shudder. "But I will try," he added, it was a short phone call.

I was nervous about calling Uncle Ron. I had some rapport with Uncle Ed, but I hadn't spoken to Ron since I had been eight years old when I had chosen him as the subject of a profile piece I had to write in school. I called to ask him about his experience of being in the Navy. He wasn't particularly warm and fuzzy back then. Calling all these years later, I didn't know what to expect. A woman answered in a Russian accent.

"Hello?"

"Hi, is Ronnie there?" There was a pause. Mom and I were probably the only ones who called him Ronnie.

"Yes, just a moment. I get him for you." He got on the phone.

"Hi Uncle Ron, it's Heather Moore, your niece."

"Well, hi. How are you?" A wave of relief. He was much friendlier than before. He was now married to a different woman and had become a Doctor of Osteopathy (DO) in an emergency room; maybe that had softened him up a bit.

"I wanted to let you know, Dad died on the 28th."

"Oh, I'm sorry. How's your mom?"

"I don't really know. I haven't seen her cry since the hospital, and she hasn't really talked about how she feels. Although, she never has done that, so I don't know. I'm getting a conservatorship over her, and I know you did that for Mam'maw (my grandmother). What did you have to do? I'm so overwhelmed. I'm settling the estate and taking care of Mom all on my own." I was dropping hints all over the place that I wanted help, but neither uncle was picking up what I was putting down.

"The conservatorship will give you the power to do anything. You can sign on behalf of your mom; you can take care of her affairs. You have to document everything, so keep good records. You'll have to take it to the court, and deal with social security at the end of each year. None of this will happen overnight. It's a long process, but it will get done one step at a time."

"Mom clearly has schizophrenia but has never been diagnosed and she needs medication; she can't live on her own. I don't know what to do. With your medical connection can you help me?"

"Mental health in Mississippi is probably among of the worst in the country," he said. "I'm sure it's much better in California. You could take her out there. Don't get your hopes up, but I will ask around for you."

I could feel tiny cracks creeping their way in around my resolve to take on this responsibility. I know it was unreasonable to ask after having no relationship with him for thirty years, but a part of me wanted my uncles to say, *oh yes, bring her here, we'll figure it out.* Clearly Uncle Ed was still hurt and angry that

Mom had disowned the family, and Uncle Ronnie didn't want the burden. But the reality was, she was sick. I sure wasn't moving her to California. Mental health care in this state is dismal, and she couldn't afford to live here anyway.

My life was consumed by the estate. I continued to work in my acupuncture practice three days a week and I had barely scratched the surface of my grieving process.

June 30th, my birthday, was fast approaching. I was not looking forward to turning forty. When I was younger, I had always envisioned forty as one of those milestone years where you have hit your stride in life, when things are settled. A husband, a house, a great career. This image was so far from my reality that it brought up feelings of failure. No man. No house. No career that I was deeply passionate about. I felt so lost and extremely flawed, watching in horror as the success boat sailed off into the sunset, leaving me on the shore labeled "defective goods." My Facebook feed streamed images of friends and acquaintances from high school all living the American Dream. But I had chosen California and pursued a very different path. The middle class doesn't exist here. In Michigan you can buy a nice, livable house for $100,000. In the Bay Area we have a saying: "the million-dollar fixer-upper." A million dollars will literally buy you a shack—no joke—or a condemned house you'd want to tear down and rebuild because it's in such disrepair. I didn't even have my own shack. I was about a year out of a terrible relationship and I'd been sober for three years. I felt like I was barely in the starting blocks to building a successful life. How was I ever going to catch up?

My friend Georgia, who I call Piggy, asked what I wanted to do for my birthday. I was so overwhelmed and shut down, I really didn't feel like celebrating. But since I was turning forty,

I thought I shouldn't sit around and mope. I suggested a trip to the Yuba.

The south fork of the Yuba River, nestled in the Sierra Nevada mountain range, was one of my favorite summer weekend destinations. I would hike about half a mile from the South Fork Bridge and then climb (or, more accurately, slide) down a steep area to arrive at some huge granite boulders edging the water. There, I would settle along the crystal-clear river's edge and bake in the sun. It's usually 85 degrees or warmer by late June and approaching 100 degrees by September. I have that area dialed in.

Piggy and I agreed to stay at an Air BnB there for a couple of days.

Once out on the land, without the usual distraction of the estate, I became aware of my deeper feelings. I was still numb and hurt. I knew I was stranded in victim energy and it felt as though there was nothing I could do about it. I simply observed my feelings, not trying to change them or make my experience different. I inflated a hot pink raft I'd brought with me and floated around on the river. The current was gentle and kind. Upstream there was a small rapid that I stayed in by holding onto a rock. Letting the water wash over me was its own sort of baptism. All the tension, stress, and resentment washed away by nature, my real home. Like a fish, when I was in the water, I was okay. Out of it … not so much.

Piggy tried to give me a nice birthday, but I was short and curt. I was impatient when she spoke to me and her happiness irritated me. I realized, too late, that I really wanted to be alone. I had been cranky to begin with but weeks of overstimulation, and having people in my space, had made me feel crankier. I needed space to breathe.

Back home, I wasn't ready to pick up the estate business again. It was the Fourth of July, so Piggy and I went to the Marin County Fair at the Civic Center Fairgrounds in San Rafael. I loved the Fair, mostly because of the animals. The baby pig races delighted me! We had given Piggy her nickname at this fair the year before. At first, I had thought pig racing was cruel but then I got to see how pampered the animals actually were; They relaxed in an air-conditioned trailer between each race, and they got treats and lots of petting. The temperature is usually in the nineties—blazing hot! When the trailer door opens they all come running out squealing, motivated by little treats. Each one has a different colored bandana, and you get to vote for the winner. It's definitely a main attraction. There is a petting zoo with farm animals, goats, cows, chickens, and sheep, and it was wonderful to touch the animals' fur and skin, to witness and feel their vulnerability and sweetness. Animals have always had a calming effect on me. They invite me into a world of connectedness and oneness that we humans miss when we are too caught up in the world of the mind and "doing."

Piggy and I spent the afternoon walking around and we enjoyed various comedy, music, and dance shows, and then watched the fireworks in the evening. As the sky lit up, I could feel Dad by my side. When I was a young girl, Dad, my cousins, and Uncle Steve would go to the Detroit River to watch the fireworks.

Hi Dad, I whispered inside. *I miss you. I wish I could laugh with you one more time. This light show will have to do for now. Thank you for loving me.*

Tears rolled down my eyes and I wept. Everything around me disappeared, leaving just me, Dad, and the explosions in the sky.

The following week I resumed somewhat normal function. I was working my regular hours in the clinic but spending a few hours a day on the phone, faxing documents, writing letters, or sending emails related to Dad's estate.

The continued misinformation I was receiving was putting me increasingly over the edge. I had a mountain of tasks to take care of and would need to fly back to Detroit. The conservatorship was moving at a snail's pace, and being 3,000 miles away was not helping. I would have to be physically present to file for the conservatorship in court on August 7.

The early morning non-stop flight from the San Francisco International Airport to Detroit's Wayne County Airport would become a routine journey over the next four months. I loved the view from the airplane. Seeing Lake Michigan caress Chicago meant I was almost there. On the descent, I admired the landscape and how it was covered in trees that looked like green lollipops from the air—oh, glorious summer! It was a beautiful sight. But not enough to compensate for everything that happened after I landed.

CHAPTER 16

BACK IN DETROIT

August 5, 2015

When I got to Mom's she was cooking dinner. Her face was ashen and sunken and she appeared to be walking and moving off balance; I was concerned. Since Dad's death, Mom and I hadn't talked much. When Dad was alive he would answer the phone and then pass it off to Mom so I could speak with her. But now she never answered when I called; when I sent emails, she rarely responded.

"Mom, I've been calling you, why don't you call me back? Did you know I was coming?"

"The phone isn't working." She had told me this in an email, but I thought it was crazy, paranoid talk. I walked over and picked up the phone. There was a dial tone on the other end.

"Mom, it's working fine."

"Well, as soon as you leave it will stop working." I took a deep breath, I hadn't even been in the house for thirty minutes, and I already wanted to punch the walls.

"Okay, I can call and have someone come out here."

"I don't want anyone in the house."

"Alright then, I guess you won't have a phone when you say it goes out. Is Uncle Steve still coming over to check on you?"

"Yeah, he comes every other week or so. He offers to go to the store, but I don't need anything. I have the car; I go to Kroger." Kroger was a grocery store a half mile away. "And I have all that food in the basement."

Some years earlier, Dad had started to stockpile food and supplies like toothpaste, toilet paper, batteries, water, light bulbs. Floor-to-ceiling shelves covered one entire basement wall and they were packed with canned vegetables, beans, fruit, pasta, and rice—anything in a can or a box. I thought it was peculiar, but I never said anything. Dad had been a Y2K "survivalist" and believed in being prepared. But there had been an impressive store of goods in our basement for well over a decade. It would take years to work through it all. I went into the basement and found that Mom had made a small dent in the arsenal. Besides milk, flour, and eggs, she really didn't need much. She would bake her own bread, muffins, and other things she could chew easily without teeth.

"So, what are you doing while you're here?"

"I have to be in court on Wednesday, I'm meeting with the realtor on Thursday, and I leave Friday morning."

"What are you going to court for?" I immediately felt angry, defensive and fearful, all at once. I had to quickly assess what I would and would not say. Gingerly, I replied.

"To get the conservatorship, so I can get access to the accounts and sell the houses and pay bills."

What I left out was that a Guardian ad Litem (GAL) had been assigned to Mom's case. A GAL is a person appointed by the court to represent a mentally ill person's legal proceedings. They make recommendations to the court based on various information, such as what had happened to bring the ward (Mom) into litigation, the needs of the ward regarding safety, treatment, or a counseling plan, and the permanent resolution that would be in the ward's best interest. I didn't tell Mom that this lady would be calling her. I was hoping she would give me a time frame so I could let Mom know a little ahead of time. I figured that, with short notice, Mom would have less time to overthink it and start freaking out.

After dinner, I just wanted to relax. Mom went into the computer room to work on something, and I laid on the couch to watch *Law and Order*. I've probably seen every episode at least five times, but it never gets old. There is always a marathon on one of the channels. I found it on TNT, snuggled up in my blanket and went into checked-out mode, AKA my safe mode.

The next morning, I wanted to go visit Dad at the cemetery. It had been more than two months since his funeral, and I hadn't seen the headstone yet. I had some toast and coffee, grabbed Mom's surprisingly long grocery list, and headed out the door.

In the car I rolled down the windows, breathed in the humid air I love so much, and turned on the radio. Detroit has the best radio stations. A few just play all-nineties hits, the music I listened to as a teenager and into college. Hip hop, Nirvana, Smashing Pumpkins, Metallica, NIN (Nine Inch Nails), REM ... the music brings wonderful memories and transports me back to a time of complete freedom. Sometimes I wish I could live forever in that time, with the wisdom I have now, of course. I know it's cliché, but truly that was my favorite time.

I arrived at Oakland Hills Cemetery in Novi. The grounds are nice, but it's literally surrounded on all sides by shopping malls and retail outlets. For some reason that was never explained, Dad's parents bought six plots when the cemetery was still in the countryside, nestled in woods, overlooking duck ponds.

I had to drive around a couple of times looking for Dad's plot—I always get lost—and I was already feeling overwhelmed and irritated. *Where is it?* Finally, I found it. You have to look for the pygmy tree, which was planted more than forty years ago but is barely more than eight feet tall. Dad's plot still had no headstone, and the grave was filled only halfway. *Did they forget about him? It's been two months! What's happening?* I knelt down and placed the yellow roses I had bought into the hole. I was just starting to talk to Dad when my phone rang. *Damn it! Can I get a second?*

"Hello, this is Heather."

"Hi Heather, this is Melinda, the GAL appointed to your mom. How are you?"

"I'm fine."

"I just stopped by your mother's house I had called a few times but never got a call back. She seemed very confused and didn't know about the conservatorship." I was stunned and irritated that Melinda hadn't called me first.

"She actually answered the door? She doesn't do that for strangers. I'm surprised she talked to you. I told her about the conservatorship and the court date. She either doesn't remember or she's lying to you."

"Is your mom schizophrenic?"

I began to share our family story with her. I hated telling this story and always felt I had to defend myself and my behavior. I ended up sobbing.

"I know exactly how you feel and how hard it is. Both my mom and sister have schizophrenia, and it is just crazy making. She needs to get on meds."

"I agree, but she won't see a doctor, and she doesn't think anything is wrong with her, so what am I supposed to do?"

"You can petition the court for an involuntary treatment. She would definitely qualify. You can go to the court today and fill out a form."

I appreciated her words and empathy, but I wasn't ready to have my mom committed. Still grieving Dad, settling the estate, and on top of that, putting Mom into a psych ward? It was all too much for me to bear.

"I'll be writing my report and have enough evidence to say your mother is incapacitated. There shouldn't be a problem. I'll be at court with you and Jennifer on Wednesday."

As soon as I hung up with Melinda, Mom called.

"I thought the phone wasn't working?"

"Who is this woman who showed up here asking me questions?"

"It's your guardian ad litem appointed by the court for the conservatorship."

"Did you know she was coming over?"

"I knew she was going to contact you, but I didn't know when."

"Would have been nice if you'd told me." I stayed silent. "Where are you?"

"I'm at the cemetery, wanted to see Dad. I'm going to the store and then I'll be home."

I managed to keep my composure with Mom, but after I ended the call I started crying, swearing, and screaming my head off. *I just wanted a simple day, an hour with Dad, a moment of peace. Instead, it'd all gone sideways with Melinda's call and visit, and now Mom is all pissed off—what a fucking shit show. How is the phone suddenly working? It's not unlike Mom to play these games.*

I returned home with thirteen plastic bags of groceries, double-bagged. I was amazed—plastic bags had been banned in Marin County for a couple of years by that point. Mom gave me the silent treatment; she was so good at that. She could go for days, and she has. As a child, this treatment had been devastating and confusing and I had felt very alone and isolated, as though I were doing something wrong. But through therapy and talking to other people about their experiences as children, I came to realize this wasn't about me and how I might be deficient in some way. It was about a mentally ill mother who had no other ways to cope with her own demons.

I got up at six o'clock on Wednesday to be at the Coleman A. Young Municipal Center in downtown Detroit by 8:15 a.m. I would be meeting my attorney, Jennifer, and Melinda in person for the first time. As I walked out of the parking garage, I looked up and there it was—the "Spirit of Detroit" sculpture in front of me. I felt a flicker of déjà vu. I walked down to the river and stood where Dad and I had stood almost exactly a year earlier, grateful for the miracle of that day.

In the courthouse, I passed through the metal detectors. The sound of footsteps echoing on the marble floor filled my ears. Dozens of people in suits rushed around, looking incredibly important. I felt small and scared. I had nothing to be worried about with our case. It was solid, cut and dry. I just had to make an appearance. But being here felt *final*. The beginning of the end of what my father had spent his whole life building, and the final revelation of the skeletons in his closet.

I went to sit in the courtroom, but no one was there. I wondered where the ladies were, and whether I had gotten the time wrong. I walked around the building and walked into the court room fifteen minutes later.

"Heather Moore, is Heather Moore here for Susan Moore?" Across the room stood a dark-haired woman, not much older than me.

"I'm here." She walked over.

"Hi, I'm Jennifer. We are first on the docket. Have a seat over there next to Melinda."

Sitting alone on the bench along the wall by the door was Melinda. She was a rather large woman in her late forties with short brown hair. She smiled and waved me over; she had a very maternal feel about her. The room was full of people at this point, and I could feel everyone looking at me. *Thank God I don't have to say anything.* I sat next to Melinda.

"Hi Melinda, nice to finally meet you."

"Hi hon. How are you?"

"Not well, it's all so surreal."

"Yeah, I know what you mean. Did you get those papers I was telling you about, for your mom?"

"No, not yet. It's all too much for me at the moment."

"It's not going to get any easier, trust me. Your mom needs help and medication."

"Are there side effects?"

"Yes, my family members experience side effects, but when they aren't on their meds they run away, talk to walls, do all sorts of crazy shit. There is usually weight gain, lethargy, a general feeling of numbness … They are not pleasant, which is why a lot of people go off them." Melinda was not helping her case for convincing me to commit Mom. The idea of Mom sitting around, staring out the window like a vegetable, was not what I wanted. I wanted her to be functional and happy. From what Melinda said, it didn't sound like that would be the case. I couldn't do that to her right now.

"I'm not ready Melinda. I need to settle the estate first."

"Okay, I understand." Jennifer sat on the other side of the room, facing us. My heart started pounding, and my mind flipped into overdrive. *Is the judge going to ask me anything? Will I even be able to speak? I feel completely ridiculous.* Suddenly a woman yelled out,

"The case for estate of Kenneth W. Moore for Susan Moore."

Jennifer, Melinda and I walked up to the podium. I felt one hundred eyeballs on me, I was frozen.

"Yes, your honor, we are here to allow Heather Moore, the daughter of Susan Moore, conservatorship over Susan's affairs," Jennifer said. "Her husband, Kenneth Moore, passed away, and Susan is not able to handle her affairs due to mental incompetency, which Melinda will provide evidence of. We have submitted all the estate and trust documents along with bank accounts, IRAs, and mortgages."

The judge started to look them over. "So, what is wrong with Mrs. Moore?" the judge asked.

"Your honor, I'm the appointed GAL for Susan Moore," Melinda said. "I spoke with Mrs. Moore and determined that she is not able to coherently understand what is going on or how to begin to manage her finances. Mrs. Moore appeared confused and exhibited signs of mental illness, although she has not been diagnosed. I strongly advocate for this conservatorship."

"Your honor, we also ask that Heather be dismissed from being present for future hearings, as she had to fly in from California to be here."

"Ms. Moore, you live in California?"

"Yes, your honor, in the San Francisco Bay area." Still frozen, stone like.

"Okay, I don't see any reason why that can't be accommodated. I will grant the conservatorship for one year. Ms. Moore, you are exempt from attending any further hearings."

That was it, a total of fifteen minutes. I was relieved and couldn't wait to get out of there. The three of us stepped into the hall.

"Okay, Heather," Jennifer said shaking my hand. "That's it. Wait here for your documents. Someone will come out of that door when they are ready. I'll be in touch."

"Call me if you need anything. I hope this all goes smoothly for you," Melinda said, her tone not convincing. I sat down and called Uncle Steve. Both he and Audra had been trying to get in touch.

"Hey Uncle."

"Hey sweetie, did Audra get a hold of you? She wants to know what time we're having dinner tonight."

"I don't know. I'm at the courthouse right now for Mom's conservatorship. We just finished. It went well and got approved. I'm just waiting for the documents. I'll text Audra and have her call you later."

"Okay, honey, see you later. I love you."

"Love you too."

I waited almost two hours. I thought they had forgotten about me. Finally, a woman came out and handed me a document. It named me as Mom's conservator, Mom as my ward—a protected individual. I had access to all of Mom's accounts, with a clause that said funds were not allowed to leave the state of Michigan, and that selling property was not allowed without court approval. Unfortunately, this was not the *official* conservatorship document that I could use to access bank accounts. I had to wait another sixty-plus days.

CHAPTER 17

LOOSE ENDS

My next stop was the Social Security office, where I passed another hour wait trying to get my mother signed up for social security benefits.

"Okay ma'am. Do you have a copy of your parent's marriage license?" *Why would I have a copy of my parents' marriage license?*

"No. Why do I need that?"

"We have to have it to prove they were married."

"You need to prove my parents were married? I have the will and trust documents right here stating Susan Moore is Kenneth's wife."

"Sorry ma'am, we still need to have the actual marriage license. I should be able to look that up in my system. Father's name and birthday?" After a few minutes he said, "I can't find your parents' marriage license in the system. You don't have access to any copies?" *Of course you can't find it, because nothing can be easy.* I wasn't about to ask Mom. For all I know she could have burned it.

"No, I wouldn't even know where to look."

"Okay, well, you're going to have to see someone else. I can't help you." He gave me a queue number, and I sat back down in the packed, noisy office for nearly two hours. Restlessness got the better of me so I got up and did yoga stretches at the back of the room near the "No Standing" sign. Finally, I heard my number. *Thank God.*

The man at the window had a pleasant demeanor and felt approachable, which was a huge relief.

"Hi, I'm Mr. Harrison." I told my story again. I wished I could just play a tape recorder. "You have a very unusual case," he said. I'd heard that at least a dozen times already, too. "I don't know how I can help ..."

"What?!" I burst into tears. "You *have* to help me. I just sat here for almost four hours! I have to get this finalized!"

He looked at me sternly. "I said I don't know how I am going to help you *yet*, but I am going to help you today. It's going to be fine Heather, don't worry. We will get this set up today."

Embarrassed that I had totally overreacted and created a scene, I realized that I had cut him off. I was so used to hearing "no, I can't help you," I had started to expect it, and with a hair trigger my guns were a-blazin'! He walked away and returned with tissues, handing them to me under the glass that separated us. I sat back in my chair and exhaled, weeping and wiping my eyes. My mind was so out of control.

We sat together for an hour. He needed a detailed explanation of why I was there, and Mom wasn't. He was quite cute and a little flirty. By the end I was so grateful for his help, my time there didn't seem so bad.

"Okay, Heather. The account is all set up. All you need to do is send me a copy of the marriage certificate and I will activate the account for you." He handed me a self-addressed stamped envelope; all I had to do was put the certificate in it.

Added to my to-do list: order Mom and Dad's marriage license from the Wayne County Clerk's office and get it to Mr. Harrison within thirty days.

Relieved at making headway with Social Security, I headed over to Aunt Pat's for another fun family dinner.

The next day I went to meet with Jeffery Packer, of the Packer Group realtors in Plymouth. He was a little younger than me and I really liked him. I shared what was going on with the estate, Mom, and the houses. We brainstormed prices and deadlines for when Dad's four rental properties should be listed. I told him that we would not list the house Mom lived in until after we moved her out. There was no way in hell she would let someone walk through the house.

It was my first interaction with someone associated with the estate that I felt good about. I could trust this man and I knew he had my back. I was relieved to feel I had an ally in one of the corners of my life.

CHAPTER 18

TENANT ISSUES

When I got home Mom asked where I had been. When I mentioned the realtor, she immediately started yelling at me.

"They better not come to the house. Did you tell them they could? They can't come until I move out." She went on and on. I yelled back, determined to not let her poison enter my ears.

"YES, Mom. I told them they can't come. Stop talking." But she wouldn't. She was relentless. I could feel the intensity of her energy pressing down all around me, beating me into submission. Dad could do the same thing. His energy was so forceful and negative and filled with rage that I would put my hands around my ears and close my eyes in the hopes I could keep it all out of my space. I felt so powerless. And the inability to protect myself had led to so many relationship issues in my adult life. I went into my room and closed the door. Mom was still talking.

I started to pack, as I was leaving the next day. Overall, I felt the trip had been successful, I was finally seeing some forward motion. I was still worried about money, as it would be at least a month before social security kicked in. Thankfully, the pension money was getting deposited monthly now, but the life insurance was nearly half gone.

*　　*　　*

When I got back to California, I contacted the Wayne County clerk to get my parents' marriage license. I told them I was on a deadline and needed it ASAP, and I paid extra for expedited service. I said Dad should have gotten the license in Wayne County and that they were married in November 1973, but I didn't have the exact date.

Two weeks went by, and I still hadn't heard from them when I noticed a refund in the checking account from Wayne County. When I called, they said they had found no record of Mom and Dad's license, so they had refunded my money.

"Why didn't anyone contact me?"

"A letter was sent out."

"I never received anything."

"I suggest you do a statewide search."

I only had ten days left to get the license, so I paid $100 for an expedited state search and found that Dad had registered their marriage in Oakland County, quite far away from where he and Mom had been living at the time, which was strange. By the time I finally got the license, I had to overnight it to Mr. Harrison since the deadline was September 7, the next day. Marriage license? Check.

Things were not going so smoothly with my father's investment properties. The tenant at the Pelham Street house in Allen Park was three months behind in her rent and unresponsive to my phone calls. My attorney had sent her a letter a month earlier warning she would be evicted if she didn't pay. Jeff, my realtor, called me and said he had gone over with an estimator, and the house had looked abandoned. There were boxes, beat up old furniture and a lot of garbage in the house and in the garage. There was a significant water leak in the bathroom, which created a dangerous mold issue; he thought it was unsafe; the house would need to be gutted and redone. I couldn't believe Dad would let this happen to one of his properties. I figured Laurie, the tenant, never mentioned the leak or maybe Dad was punishing her for always being late with rent. He'd often complained she never paid on time. The tenants were also four months behind on the water bill, which I ended up paying. Jeff told me he would speak to George, the attorney, about this but he felt we should just surrender the house back to the bank. The house needed thousands of dollars in repairs and with the tenant behind on rent payments we were deep under water on the property. I submitted paperwork for a deed in lieu foreclosure. This is an instrument in which a mortgagor (i.e. the borrower) conveys all interest in a real property to the mortgagee (i.e. the lender) to satisfy a loan that is in default and thereby avoid foreclosure proceedings.

Thankfully, this meant I didn't have that mortgage payment any longer, but it would take two months to get the arrangement approved. The agent I spoke with was very helpful and assured me there wouldn't be any issues, but my previous experiences left me unnerved: something always seemed to go wrong. The lady I spoke with was always so friendly that one day when I called, I was so moved by her kindness that I started crying. I felt like a battered woman, and she was one of the few people in the previous months who I felt sincerely wanted to help. This whole experience taught me how far a little kindness can go when someone is struggling. It had been shocking to me how most of the people I talked to were numb to what I was going through. All they did was insist I pay them a requisite amount of money or follow protocols that were inevitably incorrect. And then they were horribly rude when it turned out they had been wrong.

Since there seemed to be no sign things were going to let up anytime soon I paid for a *homa* to be done at Oneness University to clear some ancestral patterns. A *homa* is a fire ceremony, a ritual where an intention is set and prayers are offered. Mantras are recited and various items such as ghee, rice, herbs, and other offerings are placed into the fire. Through the mantras, the fire is asked to take the prayers and burnt offerings to God in order to clear negative energies and bring the petitioner's intention into reality. A homa can last anywhere from an hour to five hours depending on whether it's a group homa performed on behalf of a few hundred people or whether the homa is conducted just for you. This is a common enough practice in India, although considered somewhat unorthodox in an American setting. Similarly, most Americans aren't likely sitting around today wondering how to clear ancestral karma, but just in case you were wondering, clearing ancestral karma might cover hundreds of issues that your ancestors may have struggled with, and which have been bequeathed to you or others in your immediate family: stealing, lying, cheating, bad business practices, victim or poverty consciousness, genetic diseases … in fact, karma can impact us on every physical, mental, and emotional level. Whatever your forbears did not clear up in their own lifetimes can be passed down to you in yours. So, generally speaking, homas are a mechanism for clearing karma from your family's past, present, and future.

I had a homa done three times over the course of the ten months I was working on settling my father's estate. I also commissioned a puja—a thousand-year-old fire ceremony designed to assist with the dissolution of karma—to be done monthly, and I had friends praying for us. I figured we needed all the help and divine intervention we could get.

When I finally received the official conservator document in mid-September, I immediately faxed it off to seven different banking institutions. I could finally get accounts closed and houses sold. Even after I sent the conservator document, it had to go through a submittal and review process with each bank's estate team, which took six to eight weeks.

I continued to have problems with the credit union in Plymouth. The guy kept insisting I needed a power of attorney, and he also wanted to see Mom's ID. Thousands of dollars were going out every month and I was beyond nervous.

Finally, I couldn't take his bullshit anymore and I lost my cool over the phone.

"By a court of law, this conservator document should suffice. You met my mother! You are not, under any circumstances, going to get her ID. Close this account now. Do I need to send my attorney over there?" I screamed into the phone with a force I had never felt before, it was like my inner fire breathing dragon finally woke up. He finally agreed and closed the account, and I received the check a few days later.

Meanwhile, I was having issues with the company from which my dad had leased his car. I had initially told them I wanted to surrender the Explorer, but I changed my mind and decided to keep it so Mom had transportation. I sent them a payment of $1,500, which is what I'd been told would be required to keep the conversation going.

When I called Chase to make sure they'd received it, the woman I spoke with told me that, yes, they had received it, and that the car had been repossessed.

"What? You just told me you received the payment. Why did you repossess the car?"

"You told our service agent you were surrendering the vehicle."

"That was months ago! I called last week to let you know I was sending a payment and to not take the car."

"I apologize, Ma'am, but that's not what I have here. And in any case, you would not be able to continue to make payments because you are not the lease holder. The car would have to go back to the dealer."

"Really? This is the first time I'm hearing about that. I've talked to you guys at least four times and no one said I couldn't keep the vehicle. All you wanted was my money. Are you going to send my $1,500 dollars back?"

"No, Ma'am, the estate is responsible for paying off the vehicle." I laughed.

"You've got to be kidding me; we aren't paying $15,000. There's no way in hell you're getting any more of our money. My attorney will contact you. You can go fuck yourself." I hung up the phone and threw it across the room.

God damn motherfuckers. Everyone wants our money, but no one wants to actually help or give me the proper information. I felt so helpless. I burst into tears at the thought that Dad's beloved car had been taken and, worst of all, that it had happened on September 24th, *Mom's birthday. They took the car on Mom's birthday?* I sat in disbelief at the constant ironies of our situation. Just when I thought things couldn't possibly get any worse, they had.

I called Mom, but of course she didn't answer. I couldn't imagine what she must be going through. Did she feel abandoned? Did she think that *I* had done this to her?

The more time passed, the more powerless I felt, my mind constantly racing to figure out how I could fix all these problems. But there was nothing I could do except show up and play the part I still didn't fully understand. I knew Source/

God/Universe was with me, but I shut him out, feeling that I had to keep my defenses up. I believed if I let my guard down, even for a minute, all would unravel and crumble. I had to keep pushing through every phone call, every obstacle, every thought of defeat.

I went back to Michigan at the end of October. Since Mom doesn't answer the phone, I hadn't talked to her in about two months. Uncle Steve was still checking up on her occasionally, so my mind could rest slightly. Nervous as hell, I had also decided to research the involuntary committal process in Detroit. I wrote to the guides at Oneness University, asking them to pray for Mom. I also asked my Thursday night *satsang* group with Patricia to pray for us also. Satsang is kind of like the Indian version of church where people come together to pray, sing, chant, and support each other in a devotional service dedicated to honoring God's existence within us and around us. I had been attending this sacred gathering at Patricia's house for years and it helped me maintain a spiritual connection. Which I especially needed now.

I was shocked when I arrived at Mom's house to find that she was doing really well. I thought the prayers must have really worked. It was the first time since Dad had died that she looked and felt stable. Her eyes weren't so vacant, and she seemed energetically more engaged. We spent time cooking and going through boxes of my old belongings in the basement, determining what else I wanted to take back to California. I noticed more than half the food in the basement "arsenal" was gone, Mom had been going through it faster than I had expected. We looked through photo albums and shared memories from my childhood and Mom told me how she and Dad had met.

I loved looking at pictures of them when they were in California. I recognized all the backgrounds and felt I had stood decades later exactly where the pictures had been taken. I could feel their joy in being together and sense the laughter in their hearts as they looked at each other. These two people had been in love long before they had become the brittle parents I knew, the ones who shouted angrily at their daughter and basted their lives together in a patchwork quilt of denial, neglect, and snarling retribution. It was a marvel to see this aspect of them in brighter, more hopeful times. They had once been happy.

This visit was relaxing, which I needed, as I had to clear out Dad's entire file cabinet and decide which papers to take back and with me and which to throw in the trash. On Halloween, Aunt Pat's birthday, I went to dinner with her and my cousins. I was so grateful to be spending time with them. Growing up I'd always felt like an outsider, but Dad's death showed me that I had made up a story in my mind of them not liking me and me not fitting in. They loved me and had always wanted to be in my life. I often wonder if Mom's feelings of isolation and family rejection had rubbed off on me—another piece of the family baggage.

I had spoken with a friend's mother who was a therapist and she had said it would be difficult to get Mom committed and because Mom was doing so well, I chose not to petition the court to have her committed to a mental institution for treatment. I figured she was working through the shock of Dad's passing, and her grief, and that she was coming back to center. In the past she had alternated between periods of being okay and not okay.

It wasn't until my last day in Michigan that I went to meet with Jeff, the realtor. He had an investor who wanted to buy the three houses that hadn't yet sold. I was so happy and relieved! We hadn't been getting much interest, so we kept dropping the price and I was getting impatient. I wanted those houses gone! Over the previous months, Jeff had asked me at least a dozen times if he could send someone over to Mom's house to take pictures prior to listing it, and I kept telling him it was out of the question. Finally, he asked if he could take pictures of just the front of the house. I was reluctant, and annoyed about being pressured, but agreed. When I went back home and shared this with Mom, she got hugely triggered.

"I told you, no one can come over here. Well, now I've got to go, I can't stay here, I have got to leave. I can't stay here."

Tears streamed down my face as I watched Mom mumble to herself and take small pieces of furniture and kitchen appliances out the back door and into the yard as if moving them somewhere allowed her to move, too, safe and away from the scary realtor with the camera. Days before, I'd had the delusional idea Mom was okay. Like Dad and I had both done so many times before, I had overestimated her mental and emotional state. Lurking underneath the veneer of normal was a volcano of instability. I was speechless with helplessness. I walked into my room, finished packing, grabbed an apple, and got into my taxi for the airport.

She isn't well, and she never will be.

It was a bitter end to a hopeful moment in time.

CHAPTER 19

EXISTENTIAL CRISIS

December 6, 2015

After Dad died, I had begun questioning everything I was doing in my life. Nothing made sense to me. *Why am I living here, why am I doing acupuncture? Why am I spending time and energy with certain friends? Nothing in my life made me deeply fulfilled, and I kept sensing that I was way out of alignment.* I re-evaluated every aspect of my life. This was possibly an existential crisis: I didn't know who I was anymore.

I had been thinking about moving out of California for many years but had felt no calling to go anywhere else. I was tired of hustling all the time. My acupuncture practice needed constant attention, the cost of living was rising alongside all the tech salaries and everywhere I went, people were angrier, entitled and stressed out. Ordinary, everyday things like driving and shopping became a nightmare as I fought for parking spots and searched for friendly smiles in a desert of disconnection. I was heartbroken as my memory of 1990's California was rapidly getting destroyed along with my quality of life. What I really wanted was space and ease.

I wanted to deconstruct everything and start over. New location, new job, new friends. I'd done it twice before so I knew *how* to do it, but I was also aware that relocating by myself at age forty would not be an easy task.

I decided to check out Denver. I'd never been to Colorado and a good friend from high school lived there. I spent a month searching on Craigslist beforehand and sent my resume to a few acupuncture offices. I received a call back from one. We really hit it off on the phone, so we scheduled an in-person meeting for December 7 and I booked my flight.

When I arrived at my Airbnb in Denver, I had a strange feeling in my gut. It had started at the airport and was getting stronger as the day went by. I was not feeling a resonance at all, and thought the city was quite ugly.

I called Melanie, the woman who was to interview me, to make sure we were still on.

"Oh, are you here? I can't do it tomorrow; I actually scheduled someone else. Can we do it Friday?"

"Sure," I said, but I was baffled and stunned. "I leave Friday afternoon, so it will have to be early."

"Okay, sounds good, sorry about that." *Why would someone schedule an out-of-state interview and think that it was just tentative?*

That night, I met with my friend Megan. We hadn't seen each other in fifteen years. We were so similar in high school that we used to say we were cut from the same cloth. Nothing had changed. As we shared stories from our adult life, the parallel life experiences were remarkable.

Since I don't like cities, and living near nature is non-negotiable, I ventured out of Denver in my rental car to explore Golden, Fort Collins, Morrison, and Evergreen. I liked Morrison the best as it was filled with trees and surrounded by lakes, but it was a little too far out for a work commute to Denver.

I ventured through the Rockies, which initially brought on feelings of terror. The steep mountains butting up against I-70 messed with my peripheral vision and many times I started to hallucinate. Coupled with the extreme wind, I thought I would lose control of the car and fly off the road. The mountains were majestic, with sharp peaks and steep sides. They didn't look real. I pulled over at a scenic turnout around Silverthorne and took pictures of the mountains and Dillon Reservoir. It was beautiful, and otherworldly. *What planet was I on?* I drove past the picturesque towns of Vail and Copper Mountain, tiny little villages sandwiched between the highway and the mountain. They felt claustrophobic to me. Now I understood the term "valley fever."

Megan had recommended I go see Hanging Lake, the prize at the end of a steep, mile-high mountain climb. The trail was treacherous, filled with ice, and I kept falling. By the time I reached the top, I was covered with bruises and scratches, but the lake was magnificent, and well worth the climb. The lake is suspended on the edge of Glenwood Canyon's cliffs and it's filled with gorgeous turquoise water; there's also a waterfall and some hanging plants. I sat by the water for thirty minutes or so and felt a deep, inner peace. The place was pure magic.

My descent was marked by more slips and falls and after slipping on an especially broad stretch of ice and skinning my knee through my jeans, I couldn't help but start crying. All of this falling felt like a metaphor for the past few months—and for how I felt inside. Absolutely nothing was going as planned, and I was starting to take the constant delays personally.

My destination was Glenwood Hot Springs. The springs contain fifteen healing minerals and had been commercialized more than one hundred years ago. They were a bit too cold for me, but the mountainous surroundings were gorgeous, and I imagined I was in a little bowl of water, cupped by the hands of nature. I stayed until after dark. Once my nerves were calm, I decided I would cancel my interview with Melanie. I just couldn't see myself living in Colorado. The hurried quality and rudeness of the people reminded me too much of the Bay Area. If I was going to relocate, it had to be to somewhere with a vastly different attitude, not a lateral move.

Admittedly, one of my biggest desires in wanting to move was to find a man. I just wasn't attracted to men in the Bay Area and thought I could find "him" in the mountains of Colorado. I'd had numerous relationships by this point—most of them dysfunctional—and I'd been steadfastly working on overcoming the cycle of codependency and attraction to narcissistic men I'd been trapped in for pretty much my entire adult life. In 2014, two years after I got sober, is when I did my 30-day meditation program with Oneness University. It was a powerful opportunity to process trauma, meditate, and generally immerse myself in a grueling spiritual boot camp from which I was practically begging to be released about two weeks in. But I stayed the course and felt my prayer of being able to show up as a stronger, more empowered human being in my next relationship had been answered. Just over a year later, my dad died. So, although I felt ready to find my new life partner, circumstances had interfered. Was he in Colorado? I doubted that very much and I was angry that my trip hadn't worked out the way I'd hoped it would. I had another fight in my head with God over it. *Okay, if you don't want me to move you have to bring me a man!*

CHAPTER 20

CHRISTMAS

December 22, 2015

I was excited to return to Michigan for Christmas. It's my favorite time of year. I knew it would be bittersweet without Dad, and I wanted to be with Aunt Pat and my cousins. They helped me feel close to him. This Christmas could well be our last one together for quite some time because as soon as Dad died Mom had started looking for places to move. She didn't want to stay in Michigan and have to shovel snow by herself. Her research showed that Athens, Georgia, was one of the best places in the United States to retire so that's where she decided to land. I begged her to go to Oxford to be with her brothers, but her response was, "I hate that place."

I never could figure out why. I had met Mom's mother a couple of times and had never loved her energy. She would give her little toy poodle dog peanut butter and when he vomited it back up, as he always did, she thought it was funny. When Mam'maw divorced Papaw, she moved to Glendale, California, and my mother—who was fifteen at the time—had to shuttle between her dad in Mississippi and her mother in California. When I was five, we visited Mam'maw, and I remember going to the beach where something in my soul stirred with profound joy. I thought, "I LOVE it here!" The seed was sown. By the time I was about eight years old Mam'maw would call our house wanting to talk to Mom, but my mother refused to come to the phone. Mam'maw would say to me, "There's something wrong with your mother. You should do something about it."

I later found out that both my Mam'maw and Papaw had been distant with my mother when she was growing up, and Mam'maw had been cold and demeaning, telling my mother she was fat and stupid, so my mother understandably had very little self-confidence when she grew up. Mom's brothers were social, athletic, and smart. All three of them were very self-directed and my mom was the opposite. She was anti-social, she didn't feel she was very smart, and she never knew what she wanted to do. Mam'maw would say "your only hope is to find a man who will take care of you." Maybe it's no surprise she didn't want to go back to the scene of her childhood neglect and shame.

We decided she would move after Christmas before the New Year. She was supposed to be getting the house packed up so we would be able to move during the week I had scheduled to take off. But the anxiety of moving Mom to Athens was looming in the background as I headed back to Michigan. I was uncertain how things would transpire, but keeping the faith that it would have a positive outcome.

I landed at exactly 4:14 p.m. on Tuesday, December 22nd, as scheduled, and was greeted with typical seasonal Detroit flair. These people know how to do holidays! I stood in the airport square and let myself take it all in. There was a Santa walking around *Ho-Ho-Ho*-ing and giving out candy to scrambling, squealing kids. Christmas music was playing. Everyone's smiles exuded joy. I let out a big exhalation. *It's Christmas, and I'm home.* Tears of gratitude streamed down my face.

Boarding the shuttle to my rental car, I was greeted by a jolly, slender Black man in a Santa hat.

"Hello, I'm the Candyman. I will be escorting you to your vehicle," he said, with the hugest smile. We were packed into the shuttle like sardines, but I didn't care. I felt delighted by the sound of Christmas jazz music. I got the front row seat and could hear the Candyman humming and singing along with the music as he drove. It was a lullaby. I learned later that the Candyman was locally famous and very few people actually got a glimpse of him—he was a legend in his own way, and I felt lucky. I was struck again by the warmth of the people in Detroit and had a deeper appreciation for why Dad never moved away from the city. I was missing Dad on this, my first Christmas without him in my world. Christmas had always been a happy time in my family's life, in fact the three-month period from Halloween until New Year's was always joyful, full of decorations, great food, and cheerful company. We never fought or argued during the holidays and I still to this day love that time of year. Once I moved to California I didn't come home very often—finances were tight and for a couple of years I wasn't even talking to my father because all he did was judge me for my decisions and all I did was resent his interference. In fact, all we did was fight. Why go there? But there was still a chance this one last Christmas in Michigan could be a happy one.

When I arrived home, Mom had dinner waiting and the TV was blaring. I looked around. All of Dad's things were gone. Nothing was there that had belonged to him, except for the house, which felt like a shell. Mom didn't seem to have packed all that much of what was remaining. I went downstairs to check the basement. Nothing had been touched. It was still chock full of stuff.

"Mom, you didn't pack the basement."

"I'm not packing anything down there except your stuff. We're just leaving it."

"Mom, I've already told you. We can't just leave it." I sounded like a broken record. I abandoned my will and I resigned myself to the fact that she would never listen to me. She only listened to the voice in her head. It was pointless and I was getting worked up for nothing. I was the only one suffering. I would just ask Aunt Pat and Kelly to clear it out after we left.

Our plan was to leave on Sunday, December 27, which gave us five days to get Mom organized. I watched her behavior closely to see what I would be contending with as we embarked on our adventure South. She seemed relatively okay, still as controlling as ever. And I was still as reactive as ever. As a kid I developed dozens of conditioned reactions to my parents' behavior. I watched myself in horror as I reverted back to my teenage self, just trying to get out from my mother's control, but I couldn't do it. I was stuck in the past, a frozen child paralyzed in time. Never able to meet the moment and respond differently. And I was overcome with helplessness.

Christmas morning finally came. In the past, we'd had a huge tree with tons of presents underneath it. Our family tradition was to have stockings full of chocolate treats, toothpaste, Post-it Notes, batteries, all the myriad basic things we used throughout the year. I was excited when I woke up and ran into the living room to see Mom standing there. There were no presents or stockings. My inner child sank through the floor; this wasn't Christmas.

"Well, Heather, Merry Christmas." She handed me a card. Tears started to fill my eyes and stream down my face.

"Where are the stockings?" I asked. I opened the card. It was full of twenty dollars bills, amounting to two hundred and sixty dollars.

"I don't have a car, so how am I supposed to buy anything?"

The little girl inside of me was so disappointed, and before I could censor myself she (I) blurted out, "you could have walked to the dollar store, or ordered from Amazon, or gotten a cab! You could have done something more!"

As soon as the words came out, I felt so ashamed. Of course, I knew how utterly ridiculous the scenario I had just described was, but my little girl missed her dad and desperately wanted our traditional Christmas—not to mention that I hadn't bought my mother anything, either.

"This Christmas sucks." I stomped to my room, collapsed on my bed, and cried.

A dozen stories and justifications ran through my head about what had just happened. I tried to ignore them and just felt the despair and hurt coming up. My inability to adequately grieve the last six months was catching up to me. I was losing it. I needed all of this to be over.

Mom made pancakes, and after I composed myself, I went out to the dining room. My place was set with pancakes covered in homemade blueberry sauce—my favorite—and maple syrup.

"Sorry that I said those things to you. I know you can't go anywhere."

"I know it's hard, Heather, we're doing the best we can." I nodded my head and sighed. "We should say grace."

"Go ahead," Mom said.

"Dear God, thank you for blessing us with this wonderful food. Thank you for letting me be here for Christmas and all the miracles and blessings you have brought to us this year. I ask that you take care of Dad, wherever he may be." At this, Mom burst out laughing. I started crying again.

"Oh, I'm so sorry, that was rude of me." Mom said.

"What the hell is wrong with you? Yes, very rude."

"Heather, I said I was sorry, don't be sad."

"Why are you ALWAYS telling me how to feel? You've done that since I was a kid. STOP IT! My feelings are mine, if they make you uncomfortable then you can leave the room. Humans have emotions, Mother, it's a natural normal thing. Just because you have issues with yours doesn't mean mine are wrong." She told me to calm down and that it wasn't that bad, that she was sorry. I wanted to blurt out a fuck-you, but I left my Christmas pancakes at the table and went to my room.

It was nearly time to go to Aunt Pat's. I got myself ready and left for Plymouth. I started out excited to see everyone, especially after what had happened with Mom, but as I approached Aunt Pat's street I was overcome again with grief. I recognized that I was holding on too tightly to what had been. To Dad, the feeling of Christmas, all of it.

For as long as I could remember, Dad had bought everyone huge tins of popcorn for Christmas, so keeping with the tradition I had done the same. Holding back my tears, I grabbed the tins from the back seat of the car and walked into the house. Everyone came towards me with hugs and kisses. When Kelly came over, I could not hold it back any longer and I sobbed in her arms.

"Oh honey, what is it?"

"Dad's not here and it sucks."

"I know it does. We all miss him. Thanksgiving was so quiet. I want you to know that no one has forgotten about him. We were all at a fish fry awhile back and saw someone who looked just like your dad. I said to Dad, 'Is that Uncle Ken? It looks just like him.' I had to do a double take. And people are still talking about him and telling stories about things he did when we're out at events or other functions. He is very loved and deeply missed." She had tears in her eyes.

Kelly has a way with words and always knows the exact thing to say to make people feel better. She has an incredible gift.

"Thanks, Kel."

I set the popcorn under the tree.

When Dad died and we realized we had so few family pictures, we made a pact to take a bunch at the holidays. Audra, Kelly, Matthew, and I went bonkers with picture-taking and laughed hysterically all the while. I even made us go outside in front of the chicken coop to take pictures since at 65 degrees it was unusually warm for Christmas Day. Matthew had a selfie stick and was able to get all twelve of us in the photo. It was one of those moments where there were too many chefs in the kitchen, each talking loudly about how we should take the picture. We each had our input at the same time, and we were so boisterous no one could hear anything. The photo is perfect. The essence of each of us shines through, giving a perfect glimpse into who we are as individuals, but also as the family collective. This was the first picture taken of our entire family that didn't include Dad.

We sat down for dinner and ate the typical seasonal fare: roast lamb, ham, cabbage, fresh bread, green beans, green salad.

"How's your mom doing?" Aunt Mary asked. The room went quiet. I hated this question.

"Fine, I guess. She doesn't say much, and I still haven't seen her cry. But I can't imagine what she's going through. This will be the first time in her life she is on her own. I don't even think she's ever had a bank account."

"Well, why is she going to Georgia?"

"I don't know. I told her to pick a place and that's where she picked. I want to find a place where she can walk to the grocery store. They also have free seniors' bus service, where they'll come and pick you up, take you where you need to go."

It's been a point of pride for me my whole life that I never ask for help. I've been determined to be a lone wolf and single-mindedly dedicated to figuring things out on my own, especially since my parents had pretty much trained me to feel they were not only unable to support me but also, to a large extent, unwilling to do so. Or so my story went growing up and into my adult years. But I had concluded that it was dangerous to be vulnerable. And despite the fact I had perceptively messed up on a few fairly major success-related issues, I considered myself to be pretty damned capable. But something had changed over the past year or two. My spiritual studies combined with the path to my sobriety had forced me to look at how I was living my life and to find the places where I not only had blind spots but was being downright arrogant. The "lone wolf" approach to life hadn't created abundance and stability. It might have isolated me from the pain I perceived my parents were trying to inflict upon me, but it hadn't brought me peace or ease. Stubbornly doing everything on my own hadn't eased my burden. It had quadrupled it. What if there was another way to live my life? What if I didn't have to do everything on my own? What if I was a whisper away from support and assistance? Could it be that simple? I finally found the courage to be vulnerable and reach out.

"Can you all help me and Mom?" I asked. "I'm getting the U-Haul Sunday to leave on Monday. Can you come over and help us pack the truck?"

Danny and Uncle Steve, and then Kelly and Aunt Pat all said they would be there. I felt such relief that they weren't busy, as I had obviously waited until the very last minute to ask. After dinner we cleaned up and broke out a puzzle. We always had some activity after dinner. The men retired to the family room to watch sports, and the women played cards or did puzzles. I had been extremely good at puzzles as a kid and enjoyed them, but this one was challenging, and I couldn't get the border to come together. I was getting frustrated.

"Boy, Heather, you aren't good at this, come on," Aunt Mary chided.

"Ha! I used to be really good; I don't know what happened." What had happened was that I was overwhelmed and couldn't concentrate. My anxiety started going through the roof with the anticipation of getting a U-Haul. Could I even drive the thing? And was I actually going to be able to get Mom into the vehicle? I was going over and anticipating all of the things that could go wrong and how I would remedy them.

I finally had enough of the frustrating puzzle and decided it was time to return home and see what Mom was up to. I hugged and kissed my dear family, thanked them, and said I'd see them Sunday morning. When I got home, Mom was watching TV, and I was feeling horribly depressed, but grateful that Christmas was nearly over and I could get on with the task of moving Mom and selling the house. Mom had stacked up all the boxes in the dining room, filled with what we were taking. I walked through all the rooms. The echo from the hardwood of an empty house was further evidence of Dad's absence. I tried presencing myself by reflecting on my parents' fractured but enduring marriage. My mother's unpredictable and hurtful behavior. My father's mismanagement of his finances and his denial of my mother's mental instability. My own seething anger at the loneliness of my life. I had grown up and left home in a relentless determination to create something better for myself. Maybe finally letting go of my father could actually be the start of something more hopeful for both my mother and me.

CHAPTER 21

PREPARING FOR DEPARTURE

December 26, 2015

My alarm went off and I happily got up. *Finally, we are doing this thing.* Aunt Pat and Uncle Steve showed up first, Kelly and Dan a few minutes after. We all went inside and started taking inventory, going room to room, deciding what was going in the U-Haul and what was staying to be sold or donated. Then we walked down into the basement.

"Holy shit, you want me to pack all this up?" Aunt Pat yelled. There was a lot of stuff. The entire south wall of the house was shelving packed with food, dishes, books, craft and painting supplies. In the middle of the room was a full home-workout gym we'd had since I was a kid. And dozens of boxes. I had no idea what was in them.

"I'll have to have an estate sale, there's no way I can do this," she said. Fortunately, she ran estate sales as a side business.

"Okay, do whatever you want, I just need it to get done by the end of the week so we can list the house," I replied. Next, the garage.

Mom clicked the opener. It was the first time I had seen what was in there, as she had previously refused to give me access. We all gasped; the entire garage was packed full: tools, paint, boxes, and God knows what else.

"Ken never did throw anything away, that was common knowledge," Mom joked.

Jesus, what a mess. I felt bad that I hadn't given Aunt Pat a clearer picture of what she was getting herself into. I really didn't know how much work it was going to be. More fodder for an estate sale. Customarily she takes forty percent. I told her to keep it all.

Uncle Steve and I went to get the U-Haul. While waiting in line, I started freaking out. *What if I can't drive this thing? What if I get in an accident? What if Mom won't get in unless I let her drive?* Every possible worst-case scenario filled my mind.

When I had finished the paperwork for renting the 17-foot truck that was to take us to Georgia, I walked outside and asked Uncle Steve if he would drive it back to the house. He looked at me funny.

"I'm scared; I don't want to drive it yet," I said. I drove their VW Routan back to the house and Uncle Steve backed the U-Haul into the driveway. We started carrying boxes to pack the back of the truck first. That was the easy part. Then we got to moving the bed, sofa, TV, and other, bigger items. Soon the "I-hate-moving-and-I-know-better" irritability vibe infected everyone. Arguments broke out. Why can moving bring out the worst in people, even when it's not their own stuff?

"Why are you moving all of this? It's all junk. You could save your money with this truck and buy it all when you get there." The truck was costing a little over a thousand dollars. There was no way in hell we could buy all this stuff again for a thousand dollars. To me, these were Dad's things, and I didn't want to just throw them away.

Mom was getting on my nerves, moving from place to place, and not doing anything to help. Clearly, she was overwhelmed and, I'm sure, scared, watching her whole life get packed up in a truck. Everyone added their opinion on how things should fit and what should go in next. It was clear I hadn't rented a big enough truck. My fear of driving dictated what size we would get, and I didn't feel comfortable with the next step up, a 20-foot truck. We finally got everything into the truck except two huge boxes of food and spices; those we put in Kelly's car.

"Oh good, I don't have to go to the grocery store now," she said. We giggled.

Grumpy energy among the men was making me uncomfortable, and I felt I had to fix it, so I invited everyone to Panera's for lunch, my treat. Mom chose not to come with us.

*   *   *

When I arrived back after lunch it was almost 4:00 p.m. I was beginning to get restless, and my anxiety was kicking up again. I couldn't breathe and my mind was racing, continuing with fear-based vignette sketches of potential disasters. *None of that is actually happening at this moment*, I reminded myself. I took deep breaths and tried to connect with my heart. *I'm alive and safe and nothing bad is happening.* Mom and I hadn't talked very much over the previous week, trying to avoid bringing out the worst in each other. I took a shower and got ready for bed. The TV was already packed, and Mom was shuffling around the house. I walked into the living room to help her with a box. As she bent over, in slow motion - her glasses fell off and broke into pieces. I gasped.

Holy shit, the proverbial glasses finally broke.

Originally mine from 1985, they had been taped and re-taped. One of the arms had been re-created with paperclips.

Now it was time to let them go. For some reason, the world stood still in that moment. Mom would finally have to go see an eye doctor and get proper care. The old was breaking down and the new hadn't yet revealed itself, a pattern happening on many levels in our lives at the moment. Mom just picked the pieces of broken glasses up and we both stared at them for a few moments, before she said, "Oh well."

I hadn't unplugged the internet yet. I had to take the unit to AT&T cable in Dearborn first thing in the morning. Thankfully they opened at 7:00 a.m. So, I watched Hulu on my computer until my eyes were heavy. Mom slept on an air-mattress in the living room, and I slept on Mom and Dad's old bed, which was so beaten up it wasn't worth taking. It had established itself into a permanent taco shape. I couldn't sleep. There was a coldness inside me that I couldn't shake.

We woke up early. I had just got back from the cable store in Dearborn when Aunt Pat and Kelly arrived to get started on organizing the estate sale. Aunt Pat had listed it on Craigslist for Wednesday and Thursday. Mom stuffed the front seat of the truck with food, coats, and anything we couldn't fit in the back.

"Better get going," Kelly said. "There's a winter storm coming in, and they say it's going to start hailing soon." Danny was already out laying salt on the roads.

Shit, we have to leave. I don't want to get caught in hail. My heart was jumping out of my chest at the thought of driving the truck. *I have to do this. I can do this. It's easy.* I repeated this to myself until I believed it.

CHAPTER 22

ON THE ROAD

December 27, 2015

"Okay, we're ready," Mom said. We hugged everyone goodbye. Waves of sadness flowed through me as I felt the loss of permanently leaving Dad's house. It was another part of him I had to let go of.

"I love you guys. I'll text you when we get to Kentucky."

The drive from Redford to Athens was twelve hours. It's hard being in the car for more than four hours, so we decided to split the journey into two days. Mom and I climbed into the truck, and I went through all the necessary adjustments: seat, seatbelt, mirrors, how to work the radio, windshield wipers—all check. Mom had so much stuff packed into the front seat we could barely move. I was feeling relieved that she was actually in the truck and wasn't making a fuss about who was driving. Having thirty percent of her vision left did not give her much leverage.

I put the truck in drive and paused for a moment. I took a deep breath and took a mental image of the neighborhood so I wouldn't forget. Aunt Pat and Kelly stood on the front porch and waved. They each wore slightly worried expressions—I imagine partly because they were wondering if we would make it, and partly because they were thinking about all the cleaning and organizing Aunt Pat would have to do in the basement and garage. I took my foot off the pedal as we waved goodbye.

It took only a few seconds for me to realize that driving a 17-foot truck was easy. I had envisioned the weight would make it slow to stop and hard to see, but neither was the case. I navigated through our neighborhood and found my way to the on-ramp for I-96 West, and we were finally on our way.

Mom seemed to be okay until two hours into our drive. She was starting to get that glazed-over look, smacking her lips and talking to herself with the added distraction of random hand gestures. Any joy I had about the adventure that laid before us quickly dissolved and I wondered if this trip was going to be harder than I thought.

"So, is the house sold now? Who bought it?" she asked. I had already answered these questions at least five times.

"No, Mom, it's not sold yet. The realtor is coming over today to take pictures. Aunt Pat will give him the keys and the garage door opener." I tried to shift the conversation towards things she could get excited about. "So, what are you going to do in Athens? What drew you to that place?"

"Well, I don't want to shovel snow, so I need to be someplace warm. When I researched online it was rated in the top ten of places to retire. They have facilities and services for seniors. I just hope people don't start following me around."

Shit, delusions were emerging. She hadn't talked about being followed since I had arrived for Christmas. That's the gut-wrenchingly hard part: I would start feeling hopeful because she seemed to be doing well and I'd think that maybe *this time it will be different*. But once she got triggered, I'd fall into a grief-and-shame spiral. My own wishful thinking and my inability to want to deal with her gets me every time.

"Mom, you aren't being followed. I constantly feel like a broken record with you and it's getting so old, it's moldy."

"So, you think it's all in my head? All these years?"

"Yep."

"Yeah right. I wish you people would leave me alone." For the next hour-and-a-half she complained about everything under the sun: having no money, the state of the government, how her back hurt, how uncomfortable she was in the seat, how she couldn't see properly, on and on. I couldn't take it anymore.

"Mom, STOP! You are so negative right now I want to crawl out of my skin. Just shut up! Focus on something happy and positive. Look at the trees, the fields, the landscape, it's so beautiful!"

That went over like a lead balloon. She couldn't find anything positive to talk about, so we decided to drive in silence until I found the song, "Hard to Handle" by the Black Crowes on the radio and screamed with excitement. A way to finally move some internal energy, I started shouting along, throwing my head around, air drumming, and pounding the steering wheel. Mom began to freak out.

"Who is this? Oh Lord, what is this noise!" It felt so good to laugh.

"Just sing along, Momma, have some fun." She covered her ears while I kept laughing. That reprieve lasted a few minutes, but then the song was over and my mind took off in a million directions again. *What's going to happen? How am I going to get her into an apartment?* We could see the dark clouds in the rear-view mirror and heard on the news about the hail behind us. Rain was expected in front of us, but I could handle rain.

About three hours in we stopped for gas, food, and a bathroom break at a Pilot travel center. I was washing my hands when Mom whispered to me at the sink. I couldn't understand her at first.

"What?"

"The toilet is broken. It doesn't have a handle."

Then it occurred to me: Mom hadn't been in a public restroom since the 1980s. I felt a wave of warmth for her.

"Everything is automatic, Mom. It flushes on its own, you don't have to touch anything. Here, put your hands under the faucet, it works through motion detection."

"Oh, wow, look at that."

I couldn't imagine what my mother was going through. She had just stepped into the twenty-first century, fifteen years late. We walked to the adjacent McDonald's and ordered lunch. Mom looked so scared, she could barely order her coffee and hamburger. Clutching her purse and moving from side to side, maintaining a safe distance from the people around her. She grabbed her coffee and went to sit down. I watched her from a distance at the register and waves of compassion came over me. I felt so sorry for her. She was so vulnerable and small, like a child. I took my Diet Coke and joined her.

"How does it feel to be in the world, Mom?"

"A lot has changed, that's for sure." We ate our food and walked out to the truck which I had moved to be near a grassy area after filling the tank. The sun was still shining and it was a pleasant 70 degrees.

"Let's do some yoga before we get in the car," I said.

"Alright," Mom said. We flung off our shoes, played, and stretched in the grass. Stiff from driving, it was a relief and a delight to move around. Like when your clothes are too tight and you take them off and rub the itchy, sore red lines that have formed in your skin. Mom had never been big into yoga, but she had become interested in body building when I was young, so dad built that gym in the basement where she spent hours working out. Since then, I've known her to have always been interested in fitness generally: we had all kinds of VHS tapes—some of them yoga workouts—that she occasionally played. We both needed a chance to move after being cooped up in the truck for so long. And then we climbed back in.

Traffic remained steady until we got to Cincinnati where it started raining. I'd never traveled through Cincinnati before. We came over a hill and descended into a small valley. I was struck by its character and charm. It was quite pretty.

We were about an hour-and-a-half from Lexington, Kentucky, where we would stop for the night. Already, Mom's back and knees were beginning to hurt, and she couldn't sit still in her seat. I could feel her agitation. I couldn't wait to get there, get out, and have some personal space, too.

At this point driving the truck 80 miles per hour down the highway seemed easy.

"Don't you think you're driving too fast?"

"No, Mom, I want to get to the hotel. I'm tired and want to get out of the truck."

I could hear things shifting around in the back. *I hope it isn't a huge mess when we arrive.*

After we crossed the Kentucky border the landscape changed again. The corridor of I-75 was banked by gorgeous blue shale and limestone. We went on like that for miles, flowing through a sea of beautiful blue, backed by fields of bluegrass. Seeing the Pottsville Escarpment, peaceful and serene, we knew we had entered the South. Soft, sloping, sparsely populated hills went on for miles. Mom was quiet. My mind rested for a while, and I settled on country music. Mom likes Rascal

Flatts and others I'd never heard of and having her occupied gave me some breathing room.

I took the first exit that had a hotel in Lexington. It was 6:00 p.m., almost dark, and raining hard. I parked in the Holiday Inn lot and went inside where we were greeted by a large jolly woman with a thick accent.

"Hi, baby. You need a room for the night?"

"Yes, please, two queen beds." Keys in hand, I hurried through the rain back to the truck and moved it to the side of the building near where our room was. Mom and I unloaded the cab, now smelling of the stinky food we had brought, and garbage. We took our pillows and winter coats into our room.

When I lifted the truck's back gate, pieces of wood from Mom's hand-carved Santa Claus and other holiday decorations she had made spilled out onto the concrete. The two of us stood there, getting drenched in the rain, completely bereft: her prized Christmas sculptures, ruined. And her cherished dulcimer: a huge crack in the body. Mom looked devastated.

"We should have wrapped them, Momma. I am so sorry."

Mom grabbed her yellow overnight bag, and I hauled out my huge suitcase. We shoved the broken pieces back into the truck and went to the room. There was nothing more to say.

"Are you hungry, Ma? There is a pub next door."

"No, not really." All we had eaten was some fruit for breakfast and a hamburger and fries for lunch. Stress causes my digestion to completely shut down. I get nauseous and lose my appetite. I suspected Mom had the same problem.

"Okay. Well, I'm gonna walk over and get something." I just needed to get away from her. Too much time in her space— my nervous system was beginning to fail, screaming "Mayday, Mayday, Mayday". I walked to the bar but it was closed, so I headed to the faux café in the hotel: a fluorescent-lit room with a coffee pot and granola bars. It looked like something out of a horror film, but it was better than nothing. I took some coffee and went outside under an awning to smoke and try to get back in my body. The drive had left me totally frazzled and I couldn't relax.

I called my friend and healer, Walker, and asked him if he could give me an energy healing session. I don't really know what he does or how it works, but I always feel radically different after his sessions, frequently noticing permanent shifts in my consciousness and behavior. He said he could support me in thirty minutes. I usually went to Walker in person, but he also does remote phone sessions. I needed to lie down for the session, but I didn't want to go back to the room and have Mom's energy interfering with Walker's work on me. The only opportune spot was on a couch off the side of the entry lobby. It was quiet, but not totally distraction-free. A young man was now working the front desk. He must have thought I was crazy, just lying there on his couch. But I didn't care. I needed energetic and emotional support and if this was how I was going to get it, then so be it. I told Mom I needed to take a call and would be gone for an hour. I was hoping she would be asleep by the time I got back.

"Hey, Walker."

"Hi Heather. How is the trip going?"

"Christmas was great, but Mom and I left today, and it has not been fun. She's sliding into delusions, and I have a horrible feeling about this move. My stomach is in knots, my mind is racing, and I can't calm down."

"Okay, let's take a look." There was a long pause that felt like eternity, while he tuned into my energy field to get a full picture of what needed to be cleared. "There is a lot of interference in your mom's space. A lot of family karma, ancestors." Ancestral karma. Again.

"Okay. I'm ready." I had my headphones on and I closed my eyes, opening them every so often to curious glances from people in the lobby, who would look at me inquiringly and no doubt wonder, *Is that girl okay? What is she doing?* I felt vulnerable and wanted to hide, but I had nowhere to go. Walker's sessions last an hour, mostly in silence. When we started, I felt like a wreck. By the end, I didn't feel one hundred percent restored, but my anxiety had cranked down a few notches and I felt more aligned and grounded. We wrapped up and he wished me blessings.

Back in our room, Mom was still awake, staring at the wall. I let out a big sigh internally to myself. It was ten o'clock.

"Aren't you sleepy Mom? You should go to bed."

"Yah, I'm tired but I don't like hotel rooms. I can't get comfortable." I wanted to say *does anything make you comfortable?* She was continually fidgeting, physically and mentally in constant motion. Her inability to relax made me extremely uncomfortable and put me on edge.

"All right, I'm going to take a shower." I was worried she would go through the legal documents I had brought and take them or hide them somewhere. Her history of throwing Dad's important papers into the fireplace made me suspicious of what she might do while my back was turned.

As I mentioned earlier, Mom would refuse to sign anything my dad asked her to sign but the kicker was that she would often burn the paperwork before pretending he hadn't given it to her. I don't know if it was her illness or just spite, but she would make his life miserable for a time. They made each other's lives miserable. So, with Mom's social security card, birth certificate, and marriage certificate in my bag, along with her conservator documents and her bank statements, I had a lot at stake. If I lost any of those documents, I was screwed. I grabbed my bag, took it into the bathroom with me, and locked the door. I like staying in nice hotels, but this place left much to be desired. The bathroom was musty and damp with a lingering funk of cleaning residue. The water felt good, but I didn't feel clean after the shower. I concluded I was toxic internally from the processed food I'd been eating and the stress hormones I'd been generating. My pajamas smelled like Dad's house, reminding me again that life, as I'd known it, was over. I never thought that I would go anywhere with Mom, let alone find myself sitting in a hotel room with her in the middle of Kentucky. I was in complete shock. I felt like I was outside of myself watching a bizarre film, thinking, *this can't really be happening.* I was aware of how disassociated I had become. The emptiness I felt had no bottom.

I came out of the bathroom and Mom was still dressed in her street clothes, clutching her purse to her chest and staring up at the ceiling. *Is she going to snap out of this? I can't possibly find her a place while she's in this condition.* I had to keep myself in a certain pattern of denial to keep going. *It's all okay,* I told myself.

The sound of Mom continually smacking her lips amid the uncomfortable silence triggered my rage again. I flipped on the TV to drown out her smacking and pulled out my laptop to start searching for apartments. I hadn't really had time to do this earlier and our exit from Detroit had been more like an emergency escape than a planned move. The apartment situation in Athens, Georgia, was not looking very hopeful. Only a few places were available to look at in the next week. This shouldn't have surprised me. And it did. Athens is a small college town and apartment availability ebbs and flows with the school term schedule. We were arriving just after Christmas and it would likely be months before there would be a good selection of apartments to choose from. But I was used to looking for apartments in big metropolitan areas with a seemingly endless supply of apartment rentals. I hadn't factored in the reality that smaller centers have fewer apartments to choose from. Finding Mom a place to live was going to be harder than I had thought.

Mom finally fell asleep. Still fearful that she would snoop around and try to take the legal documents that proved she was actually a human being, I brought them under the covers with me. I closed my eyes and prayed that we would find a place tomorrow that would be a halfway decent place for her to live, and that Mom would be functional enough to sign a lease. I worried until I couldn't worry anymore and then fell asleep.

CHAPTER 23

KENTUCKY TO GEORGIA

December 28, 2015

It was still dark outside when all the noise Mom was making woke me up. She was stomping around, mumbling, repeatedly zipping and unzipping her bag. *What the hell?* It was still two hours before my alarm, set for seven was due to go off. I peeked over my bed covers; Mom was still in the same clothes from the night before. I don't think she had taken a shower. And she had her coat and shoes on.

"Morning, Mom."

"Yeah, get up, I want to get going. I don't like it here. I hate hotels."

"It's only five o'clock. Can I sleep another hour? Why don't you go get some coffee?"

"No. I want to go." She sat on the edge of her bed staring at me. *Are you serious?* It occurred to me that I am really good at doing things I don't like or want to do; whether it's out of obligation, responsibility, or from not wanting to be an inconvenience to other people. Mom, on the other hand, reminded me of a petulant child. I was irritated that she couldn't just bear her own discomfort and let me sleep another hour. I huffed and got up, dressed, gathered my things, and we went to the truck. The cab smelled like ripening food.

"Mom, we aren't going to eat all of this. We should have left it in Michigan. I'm taking it to the front desk lady."

The sun was barely coming up, a light glow in the distance. I entered the lobby with two shopping bags full of fruits and vegetables.

"Well, good morning, honey!" said a plump, middle-aged southern woman who greeted me with a warm smile. I was so envious of her joy that I felt a little irritated. I couldn't help the gruff tone I responded with.

"Good morning. I need to check out, and I want to give you and the staff this food. Mom and I are traveling from Michigan to Georgia and we can't eat all of it." She lit up like a Christmas tree, as if I'd just given her the best gift ever.

"Well, bless your heart! Are you sure you don't want this? Oh, my, look how delicious and fresh this looks. Y'all have great food up there in the North." I chuckled.

"We do, at times, yes."

"Okay, honey, thank you so much! We are excited to have this." She put the bags on a ledge behind her and started typing on her computer to print a receipt.

"Why are you going to Georgia, honey? That's a long drive from Michigan."

"The drive isn't so bad, the landscape is beautiful. I'm moving Mom there."

"Oh, how exciting!" she said, handing me the receipt. "Where are you from?" She held up her hand like a mitten; she wanted me to point to where I was from.

For real? I paused before responding.

Reluctantly, I touched her hand where Detroit would be. We're from Detroit. Southeastern Michigan, close to Ohio."

"You have a safe journey now. And good luck to you."

I walked out wishing I could be like her. It seemed like nothing could ever bother that woman, she took everything in stride, genuinely happy to be alive. *I'm so jaded and cynical, I've spent years of my life contemplating how I could kill myself.* I'd first thought about suicide when I was a child, with a mother who was not loving and kind at all, but who would accuse me of following her around. She would blame me for her hallucinations or sit on the couch staring vacantly out the window, ignoring me entirely. I hated school—I didn't like my teachers, and I got picked on a lot. By the time I was eleven, I wanted to die. I felt lonely and defective and invisible. Nobody seemed to care about me, and nobody picked up on the signs that might have led to someone finding out what was going on at home. Joining the color guard in the high school marching band really did save me. It gave me a place to go, a place to belong, and a circle of friends. It gave me a purpose and it brought kind adults into my life who helped me feel good about myself. My addictions had been a way of self-medicating, keeping my overwhelming emotions and shadow in check and, also, a way of flirting with death. When I began focusing on my spiritual self and then finally got sober, I felt optimistic that at some point I wouldn't feel so defective. I can't say it's been a straight line, more like the peaks and valleys of the Rockies, full of hope and full of despair.

I was grateful I met that lady that morning. She spread some sunshine over my cloud-covered mind.

When I got to the truck Mom was buckled in and ready to go. I put our destination's address into the GPS and we were on our way.

"We should get to Athens around two or three this afternoon. Are you hungry?"

"Yeah, I'm a little hungry. Would like some coffee." We stopped quickly and picked up coffees at a Starbucks. A little over an hour later, the landscape changed again. We entered Daniel Boone National Forest and even from the highway we could see it was exquisitely beautiful. Despite it being January, the trees were still glowing red, orange, and yellow for as far as the eye could see, amidst rolling hills. There was rarely a building in sight, except for the occasional gas station, and there were very few travelers on the road.

Mom was quiet, so we just drove and enjoyed the calm. Before I knew it, we were in Tennessee; the Daniel Boone Forest ended, and another began. We crossed rivers and valleys. I was in awe of the open space and grateful to the stewards before me who'd had the foresight to create national parks and land trusts. My mind started wondering. *What is happening amongst all the trees? What animals live there and what are they doing? Are there areas in these woods where humans have never walked? Are they pristine and untarnished? Our species is so intent on destroying everything and squeezing every last resource before it's left for dead.* It felt good to just let my mind wander.

We continued south towards Knoxville and passed the western edge of the Smoky Mountains. We saw signs for Chattanooga, where Great Aunt Jane, Mom's aunt, had lived most of her life as a nurse. I only met her when I was eight, but she was the matriarch of the family. At least once a month everyone in the family—nieces, nephews, second nieces and nephews, brothers, sisters, cousins, around thirty or so people, including me—would receive a letter from her. Audrey Jane Perry had been the first woman to attend Vanderbilt University. I can't imagine the resistance and sexism she had to overcome to achieve her degree at a time when very few women earned degrees. She never married, spending all her free time in church or with family. She knew what was going on with everyone in the family and would share our news in letters that were often ten or twelve pages long. I wrote back, until I was a teenager and family became the least of my interests. I had some of those letters still tucked away.

As we crossed the state line into Georgia, we saw signs for Dalton, where Mom's brother, David, used to live. We had spent Christmas with him when I was eight, on the same trip as when I met Aunt Jane. I remember how beautiful Uncle David's place was, with a creek running next to the house. I didn't care much for my cousins at that age. I fought with Brian, the oldest of three who was one year older than me. That was the last time I had seen them.

"Do you ever think about David?" I asked Mom.

"Yeah, sometimes. It's so sad." Uncle David died in 1998. Mom, of course, didn't go to the funeral, although I'm sure her family tried to contact her. Thankfully, I saw Uncle David when I was nineteen when I drove down to Atlanta to try my hand at modeling. Aunt Jane had given me David's number and I'd called to let him know my boyfriend and I were coming. We stayed with him and my Aunt Carolyn for a couple of days. It was really sweet to spend time with them. That's when I learned that Papaw had died. Uncle Ed had tried to get hold of Mom repeatedly, even sent a police car to the house to see if we still lived at the address they had for us. We were all still there, but Mom ignored Uncle Ed's efforts to communicate.

We passed a sign that read, "120 miles to Atlanta." It seemed to be the first time Mom noticed where we were and she reacted with instant suspicion.

"Why are we going to Atlanta?" She screeched and bolted up in her seat. "This isn't the way to Athens. Where are you taking me?"

"Yes, Mom. To get to Athens we have to go through Atlanta."

"No, we don't! Where are you taking me?" Her paranoia was matched by my irritation.

"Mom, look at the GPS." I yelled and handed her my phone. She looked at the map on the screen and the directions. There was a pause.

"Oh. Well, I'll be. I didn't know we had to go through Atlanta." The paranoia diminished like a tide going out, leaving behind only wet sand. I was still shaking inside.

"Where did you think I was taking you?"

"I don't know."

"If you don't trust me, Mom, then this isn't going to work."

"Okay."

I grabbed the phone back and focused my attention on the road. To physically be passing through the regions of my mother's family made the drive feel even more poignant. Getting close to the ghosts of our ancestors and the possibility of understanding why my mother was so mentally ill stimulated questions in my mind. Questions that might never be answered. *What secrets were they hiding? Why did everyone ignore what they all knew? Did they ever think about Mom, over the thirty-plus years she's been gone?*

"My back hurts!" Mom yelled. It was the tenth time she had said it, and now she was squirming in her seat, mumbling to herself, and waving her hands around. I felt so angry! Angry that she had a disease I felt powerless to do anything about, angry to be robbed of a mother, angry that my yelling couldn't change anything, even though it felt like if I just yelled enough, she might come back to me normal, rid of this horrible illness.

"Who are you talking to?" I yelled.

"What?"

"Mom, you're mumbling to yourself and waving your hands around. Who are you talking to?"

"Oh, I don't know. I didn't realize I was doing it. Myself I guess."

"Well, stop it, you're driving me nuts and it's distracting."

"Oh, my aching butt. I'm so tired of sitting."

"We only have a couple more hours."

Traffic through Atlanta wasn't as bad as I expected. Before I knew it, we were on the 154 towards Athens, just forty-five minutes to go. A decade earlier I had visited a college friend who was going to graduate school in Athens. I remember it being a lot lusher and greener. Now it seemed remote and dusty.

The long corridor along 154 to the 20 seemed to take forever. Mom was excited that we were almost there and liked the landscape.

"You can take a bus into Atlanta, Mom."

"Why would I ever want to go to Atlanta?" she hissed. Nothing I suggested was ever met with delight or possibility, she always responded in a negative tone that made me feel like I had said something ridiculous.

"Well, maybe you'll want to see a show or something."

"No, I wouldn't want to do that." I sighed and dropped the topic.

CHAPTER 24

ATHENS, GEORGIA

We entered Athens on the northwest side off Highway 8 and onto Prince Avenue, which appeared to be a main thoroughfare through the city. I had written down the name of an apartment complex that had seemed nice online, and we stopped there first: Red Oak Village. It was a gorgeous community, with new apartments and not just students as tenants. There were professionals and families there, as well. I parked the truck, in total relief to have finally arrived.

"This looks really expensive." Mom said. "I can't afford this."

"Mom, there isn't much available, and you can afford this. I think its $1,200 a month.

"Oh, I don't know if I like it. It's also far away from the store."

"Mom, they have transportation for seniors. All you have to do is call. We're here now, so we might as well go in." She slowly got out of the truck and followed me. The office was huge and lavish, with tall windows, a fireplace, and antebellum-style architecture. A young woman greeted us.

"Hi. My mom is looking for an apartment to rent." Mom was lingering about ten feet behind me, near the entrance lobby.

"Okay, I just need to get some information from your mom." Mom walked closer, clutching her purse. "I'm Jessica. Can I see your driver's license ma'am?"

"Why do you need to see my driver's license?"

"We need it for legal reasons." That was hardly a good enough answer for Mom, who hesitated, but handed it over.

"What kind of apartment are you looking for?" Jessica asked brightly.

"A two bedroom, ideally," I said. Jessica nodded and started typing on her computer. Mom and I walked around the lobby. The foyer was gorgeous, with fifteen-foot, floor-to-ceiling windows and beautifully tiled floors. It was solidly constructed and everything was brand new.

"This is really nice, Mom. What do you think?"

"This is too expensive," she whispered. "I can't afford this."

"Mom, you don't even know yet how much it is."

We walked back into the main office.

"Ma'am, may I have your social security number, please?"

"Are you done with my license?"

"No, not yet, ma'am. I have to make a copy."

"No, you don't." Mom said sharply, her voice rising as she physically stepped around the counter to stand next to her. "I want my license." Jessica stopped typing and looked from her to me, her mouth agape. I'm sure she thought Mom was going to lunge at her.

"I'm not interested in this place," Mom said sternly. "Give me my license."

"Yes, ma'am," Jessica said, handing it to her as she stood up, taking a step back to put the desk between herself and Mom.

I wanted to scream but I felt paralyzed. Mom walked right past me, clutching her purse, chin set, eyes darting left and right, focused to narrow slits as she headed for the door.

"Why does she need my license?" she muttered. "These people are going to follow me around."

I stood in shock for a moment, unable to move. I glanced at Jessica and closed my eyes, sighed, and followed her back to the truck. My ears were ringing.

"Mom, I don't have a lot of time here. I cannot spend a month looking for a place. What do you want to do now? I already told you. There aren't many places available." It was the middle of the school year in a college town, the worst time to be looking for an apartment.

"Let's go to the library, they are supposed to have resources for seniors." Mom thought she would pay $400 for an apartment. GPS said the library was just a couple of miles away. I was driving the truck hard to try and relieve my aggression and anger; things were falling and shifting in the back. Thankfully, the library parking lot was spacious with very few cars in it, and I easily pulled into a spot. The three-story library itself was unexpectedly large, and we walked up to the second floor for guest services. I waited for Mom to ask for what she needed but she stayed a few feet behind me, like she was using me as a shield. I turned.

"Well, are you going to ask?" I said.

She motioned her arm. "No, you go on and ask her." I let out a big sigh and rolled my eyes.

"Do you have any resources for seniors like housing, transportation, amenities they would need?"

"No, we don't, but you can search online." I stood there baffled. *Yes, I already know I can do that, but the public library doesn't have info for seniors? How many sixty-five-year-olds know how to effectively use the internet?*

"Okay, thanks," I said. We walked to a computer terminal, and both stood there, next to the chair.

"Are you sitting down, Mom?"

"No, you are."

"Are you helpless? I'm not going to be here to do all this for you."

My voice began to escalate and about twenty or so people at the computer stations around us all stopped what they were doing and looked at us. To avoid further argument, I sat down. "What do you want to look for?" I asked through clenched teeth.

"Okay, look for senior's housing." Everything that came up she rejected. It was fruitless. I was beyond frustrated.

"Who told you there was senior information at the library, or that Athens was a great place to retire? They have nothing for older people."

"Well, I Googled 'best place to retire' and Athens came up."

"Well, it's clearly not for handicapped or low-income people, because there is nothing here for that demographic. I guess you can retire here if you are well, able-bodied, and have money. This is a college town, bottom line." All this was done with her hovering over my shoulder waving her fingers.

"Scroll here," she points. "Okay, now Google senior low-income housing."

"Are you sure you don't want to sit down? You are making me want to scale the walls. You don't qualify for low-income housing." After twenty minutes or so I gave up. I had one other place on my list that I had looked at in Redford before we left. It was a little out of town, and before we even got there, Mom rejected it.

"This is too far out. I can't live here."

Rage, fear, and grief were starting to bubble over. I felt like I was drowning, my head just barely out of the water, gasping for air, right before I would lose consciousness.

"Mom, you are going to have to make some sacrifices on what you want right now. You can always move in six months. I have told you at least a dozen times now: I don't have a lot of time. I need to get home and go back to work."

"Okay, well, just take me to a homeless shelter then."

"What?" I could not believe she said that. "I am not taking you to a homeless shelter." She continued babbling her story about how people were following her around and she had no money. I couldn't take it anymore and I let out a blood curdling scream. We came to a stoplight and I wailed and moaned, gripping the steering wheel like it was her throat, and I could choke her to death. I wanted to punch something until I had some relief from the overwhelming sensations running through my body, until I felt like *I* wasn't choking anymore.

CHAPTER 25

THE SEARCH FOR AN APARTMENT

"Do you hate me, Heather?" Her tone was unnaturally low, almost inhuman. It felt like a demon was asking. A chill ran deep inside my body, and I felt my life was in danger.

"Do I hate you? What kind of question is that? I'm here, aren't I? You have no idea what I've done for you the last seven months. If it wasn't for my help and sacrifice, you would be homeless." Knuckles white on the wheel, teeth clenched, I half-growled, half-screamed. "I need to get out of this fucking truck!"

I felt like a caged creature whose only desire was to destroy something. I felt like I had felt at age eleven when I took apart the rusty swing set in my backyard with my bare hands. I'd been depressed and suicidal and raging against my life, my mother's weirdness, my father's determination to abandon me to my mother and her unpredictable behavior, and both parents' lack of empathy. My aloneness. My sadness. All the work I'd done on myself over the past ten years hadn't given me superhuman abilities to cope with my mother, in fact, I was becoming aware that it had kept my trauma trapped in my subconscious. My prefrontal cortex wasn't able to maintain control due to the overwhelming physical sensations I was feeling. I lost all sense of time, and I felt trapped, with no past, present, or future. Every part of me was in survival mode, trying to defend myself and create a space of safety, which I could not do. I defaulted into self-loathing and self-harm. All the ancestral clearing I'd done hadn't enabled me rise above the tidal waves of crisis that arise when sitting beside a mentally ill parent who is all take and no give. My connection to my God was tenuous right now: I felt alone, isolated, and barely able to suppress the tortured emotions my mother triggered in me. Anger. Frustration. The unfairness of the situation. It all came boiling up and I didn't want to do this anymore. Didn't want to be her caretaker. Didn't want to deal with her self-righteous paranoia and her rude determination to have her own way.

But what were my options?

We had hardly eaten for the past two days except for fast food and what was available at gas stations. I hadn't wanted to take the time to stop for a proper meal while we'd been on the road, I'd just wanted to get down here. We had pretty much exhausted our options for the day—it was approaching 4:00 in the afternoon and apartment rental offices would be closing for the day soon. I Googled hotels, and they were all $100 or more; Mom didn't want to pay that much. She was aghast at how expensive things were. Mind you, she hadn't paid for anything herself since sometime in the 1980s.

It didn't get good reviews, but the Microtel was $60 a night and right next to an Enterprise rental car; further down the street was the U-Haul dealer. We drove up a large hill into the parking lot, it was empty. I wondered if they were even open. Mom waited in the truck while I walked inside. There were two twenty-something girls, feet propped up on the counter as they texted and watched the TV that hung from the wall. No brainer why this place got only two stars. One of them lazily put her feet down.

"Hi, can I help you?"

"Yes. I need a room for two. Two beds. Just one night." She grudgingly found me a room and handed me the key. I went back to the truck for Mom and our bags and went to our room, first floor down the hall on the left. The smell was worse than it had been the night before. Musty with vinegar, I wanted to gag.

"I'm going to the rental car place." Mom started to follow. "Oh no. You stay here."

"No, I don't think so. C'mon, I don't want to stay here by myself." *What, are you afraid of—the boogie man?*

I desperately needed to get away from her; I was about to implode.

"Fine." I sighed. My frequent heavy sighs were a way for me to relieve internal pressure, but they had stopped working. We walked across the parking lot, me in front, Mom three steps behind. I walked inside and Mom waited outside, pacing the front entry stoop.

"The cheapest car, please," I said. Here was another young twenty-something, but she was very cheerful and seemed to sincerely like her job.

"How are you today? Are you visiting?"

"Yes, just arrived. Moving my mom here from Michigan."

"Oh, quite a change in weather," she said in the sweetest southern drawl I've ever heard. "She will love it!"

"Yeah, I hope so." I worked retail for many years and could recognize silent suffering. I don't know if she saw mine, but like the lady in Kentucky, she gave me positive energy that I desperately needed—which is a good reminder for anyone who works in retail that your demeanor can make a huge difference to your customers, whether you realize it or not.

With keys in hand, I walked outside. Mom and I got into the car and drove to Panera's for dinner. The afternoon was wearing on.

"So, what do you want to do, Mom?"

"Well, I think you should just take me to the shelter or the police station."

A shock of fear jolted through my body.

"What are you talking about?"

"Well, I know you need to leave, so you should just take me someplace and drop me off."

"And what are you going to do with your stuff?"

"Well, I don't know. I guess I'll just have to leave it. Can you drop the truck off with the stuff in it?"

"Are you kidding me? No, Mom, you can't just leave your stuff in the truck." I could barely eat my food. I wanted to throw up and scream the loudest scream I could muster. Holding myself together seemed nearly impossible. I was writhing in pain on the inside and never thought I would get comfortable again.

As Mom finished her dinner I sat and stared out the window. *Please, dear God, guide me. I have no idea what I'm doing here or how this is going to go, but please, give me some relief.*

After we ate, we went back to the hotel and I got online again. I turned on the TV to drown out my internal screaming. I only found three places available immediately. I called and made an appointment to see one of them the next day.

The next morning, I woke up with a horrible headache and took some ibuprofen. Mom was already dressed and ready to go.

"Hey Mom, did you sleep?"

"No, tossed and turned. Couldn't get comfortable. I'm ready to go." *Of course you are.* I got dressed and looked up places to have breakfast. Big City Bread Café looked relatively healthy and like a place I would go to at home, so we went there. I liked that it was in a small, quiet neighborhood. There were not many people there. We ordered toast with poached eggs and decaf double espresso long pulls. The food was so good! I savored the homemade jam and a very good espresso. We sat by the window, looking out on the patio at the trees, watching the rain.

It was nice to experience the rain again. I always longed for a good thunderstorm.

"There's a place we should go look at. An apartment complex close to shopping."

"Okay," Mom said so softly I could barely here it. *If she pulls another, 'this is too expensive,' I will lose it.*

I called University Garden Apartments but no one was there yet, so we drove out to another place. It was too far away for Mom, so we drove around town for a bit. We drove past the university, some theaters, and shopping complexes.

I listened to Mom daydreaming out loud, mumbling all the things she would do while she lived here—take a master gardening class or find a job working in a garden.

I called the apartment complex again.

"Hello," a woman with a European accent answered. "University Garden Apartments. This is Ingrid."

"Hi Ingrid, this is Heather. I'm interested in the two-bedroom apartment you have for rent. It's for my mom."

"Oh, great. Yes, come on by."

The apartment complex was located on Baxter Street, opposite a large shopping center, with a Fresh Market, Kroger

Grocery Store, Talbots, other clothing stores, a theater, and a Home Goods. Everything Mom needed was down the street with easy access to public transportation. It was perfect. We pulled up to the office, went inside, and met Ingrid.

"Let me grab the keys," she said. "We have coin-operated laundry and a gym next door. When are you looking to move in?"

"As soon as possible."

"Okay, great." We walked outside and went right onto the sidewalk, passing the laundry facilities. University Garden Apartments was a large complex, running many blocks along Baxter Drive. The initial apartments in the community were beautiful and had been recently remodeled. Further back into the complex, they were older and run down. Mom's unit was in the very last cluster in the complex on a cul-de-sac. We walked into the bottom unit. I immediately smelled mold. It seemed that Ingrid had turned on the air-conditioner just before we arrived; if she had hoped to mask the smell of mildew and old paint, it didn't work.

"It's a really large space," said Ingrid. "Take a look around. I'll wait outside." The front door opened into the living room with three shades of brown shag carpet and circa-1970s windows that did not close all the way. On the right was a large bedroom with a huge walk-in closet that had strange angles to it, almost like a tetrahedron. The master had its own bathroom. To the right of the living room was a large kitchen with a door to the outside. A small hallway led to another bathroom and bedroom, with ample closet space throughout. Ingrid was right. The place was very spacious. Despite the smell and outdated features, I liked it.

"What do you think, Mom?"

"It's alright."

"You have a ton of storage for all your tools, and space to sew. You could set up a great workshop in here."

"Yeah, I suppose. Well, I know you need to go, so I guess it will do."

Relief swept over me like a bucket of water on a hot day. We went outside and told Ingrid we wanted to fill out an application. When we got back to the office, I was even more surprised that Mom was amicable and sat next to me. I gave Ingrid all of Mom's pension and social security information to show her income and filled out the app for her. I handed Ingrid the completed paperwork with a $25 check for the app fee. *Is this really happening? Oh, thank God, this will be over soon.*

"When will we know if we have it?" I asked.

"I'll run the credit check ASAP, and we should know this afternoon."

"Great. Thanks so much, Ingrid. I'll wait for your call."

We drove back to the hotel and waited. Mom was restless and moved about the room talking to herself and doing what she does. I tried to ignore her and worked on my computer. I searched for apartments, just in case this didn't work out. The smell in the hotel room was making me nauseous. *Does everything in the South smell like mildew? Nothing ever dries. Ugh. So gross.* I felt like I needed to scrub my insides. I went outside to smoke.

"Hi," I said as I was passing by the front desk. "I paid for another night early this morning, but we may not need it. If we don't use it, can I get a refund?"

"No. Sorry."

The same girls from yesterday were at the front desk and today they had a few friends over. They were treating the place like their living room, eating pizza and watching TV. Irritated,

I wanted to say, *'no one is here, could you at least have given us a room that was bright and didn't smell?'* But I huffed instead and walked outside.

It was raining hard. I sat and listened to the hum of a huge air conditioner off in the distance. I gave thanks that I would be able to go home soon. I called a friend and passed an hour or so talking on the phone. It was approaching two o'clock and I hadn't heard from Ingrid yet. Fearing something must be wrong, I called.

"Hi Ingrid, this is Heather. Do you have an update on Mom's application?"

"Well, since your mom has no credit history, and the mortgage was in your father's name, I need to have evidence of payment since he passed." *Are you kidding me? I just can't get a break with this. Always an obstacle to overcome. How can I make this happen ASAP?*

"Okay, how about we call the mortgage company and do a three-way call?"

"Oh, alright. I think that will be okay."

"Hold on, let me call them." Thank God I brought all the paperwork and had the number for the mortgage company. I had the number in my file under the label: "Yes, Mom actually exists and here is the proof." I dialed and got a rep from Nationstar.

"Hi, this is Margaret. How can I help you?"

"Hi Margaret, this is Heather Moore. Can I give you my account number?"

"Yes, ma'am." I gave her the number. "Okay, give me a moment to bring up your account. Okay, here it is, on Brady Street."

"Yes. I'm calling because I've moved my mom, Susan, to Athens, Georgia, and we are searching for apartments. We found one, and they need proof that she has paid her mortgage. Can you offer some assistance? I have the apartment manager on the other line."

"Oh yes, I can speak with them."

"Great." I pressed join caller and the three of us connected. Ingrid asked Margaret a few questions and it was wrapped up in a couple of minutes. Margaret hung up.

Ingrid said she had to get the supervisor's approval and that she would call me back.

"Thanks, I want to move in today if possible. I need to return the U-Haul."

"Shouldn't be a problem."

Relieved, I hung up.

Ingrid called a little over an hour later and said we could come and sign the lease.

"Let's go, Momma. We can sign it." We walked out into the parking lot about to get into the rental car and Mom turned to me.

"Why don't you just take me to the homeless shelter?" My heart sank and my face flushed.

"We aren't doing this again Mom. What do you expect me to do with your stuff?"

"I don't need any of it, just drop me off somewhere." I lost it, I started to scream and cry.

"MOM! I am not leaving you here. I love you! I'm not just dropping you off somewhere. You have a place to live, now get in the car." She started grabbing me to hug me.

"Okay, sweetie." I wanted to throw up. I struggled to keep the thought to myself, to not say it out loud. *I don't want you to touch me and the way you say sweetie makes me want to crawl out of my skin.*

We drove over to the office, and I put the car in park.

"I'm not signing this lease. I'm not going in. I don't want it." I looked at her, feeling completely helpless and powerless.

I took my paperwork inside with tears flowing down my face.

"Hi, Ingrid."

"Hi there. I have all the paperwork. Are you okay?"

"No, Mom is not well, and she won't come inside. Can I please sign for her? I have the conservatorship paper that legally allows me to do so."

"Yes, that should be okay."

"Great, thanks." It took about twenty minutes to sign all the documents, and I handed her a check for first month's rent and the security deposit, almost $900. She handed me the keys and I walked out. I got in the car.

"We're moving you in. I have to get the U-Haul back today."

In fifteen minutes, we were back with the truck. We were moving my mother in whether she liked it or not.

CHAPTER 26

FIRST NIGHT IN MOM'S APARTMENT

Mom didn't look well. She was super pale and both of us were beyond exhausted. She started unloading boxes. As we worked, we began to realize we had to unload the couch, the dresser, the bookcase and the beds. Neither of us had the strength, so I went and knocked on the door of the neighboring apartment. It belong to two guys in their twenties who I'd seen earlier. They looked fit for our cause. One came to the door.

"Hi, I'm Heather, and my mom is your new neighbor. I'm wondering if you would be willing to help us unload some heavy items. We can't do it on our own."

Pot smoke was wafting out of their apartment, and I could see they were entertaining young women.

"I'll buy you some beer, or whatever you like." They were not thrilled with my request, but they came out and did it anyway. We moved the remaining furniture into the apartment in fifteen minutes, no doubt saving Mom and I countless hours.

When I brought in the last box, Mom was writhing on the couch.

"Oh, I don't feel good. I think I'm going to be sick." I felt no sympathy.

"Well, get to the toilet, I have to get the truck back. It's 6:45 and they close at 7:00."

I jumped in the truck and drove like mad to get to the U-Haul office and ran inside. It was 6:55.

"Hi, I'm dropping off a truck, and I just realized I didn't sweep it out or fill the gas tank. I'm so sorry. And a few Christmas bulbs were back there, shattered into a million pieces, made a big crunchy mess."

"That's okay, we'll take care of it."

"Oh my God, really? Thank you so much." Any little kindness my way felt like a miracle, and I was grateful.

A man came out of the office in back and after I realized he was on his way out for the day I convinced him to take me back to the Microtel. When I got there I grabbed our bags from our room and signed out. I drove back to the apartment in the rental car. Mom was still on the couch, light off, fan on. It was hot inside and a total mess. I had to make passageways through the clutter of the move to the kitchen and bedrooms.

"Why don't you go lie down on the bed?" I made her a little pallet on our only bed and made myself a nest in the other bedroom with a bunch of blankets and pillows.

I had emailed an SOS to another healer friend, Lokpal, asking for an emergency session that night. I settled into my nest and shifted my focus from the outer chaos to inside. Focusing on my inhalation and exhalation gave temporary relief from the insanity I was feeling. I opened Zoom at our scheduled call time and saw his shining face. My heart melted and for the first time in weeks, I felt safe. I shared with him all that was happening. He listened attentively, then paused with eyes closed. Then he nodded, opened his eyes.

"You have to let your mother go, Heather. She is not your responsibility. When you let your mother go, it is a very real possibility you may never see her again. You have to shut the door and claim yourself. You have to take care of yourself. You've been taking care of her energetically your whole life, at the expense of you. If you want fulfillment and happiness, you have to let her go."

He continued to speak but I didn't hear anything he said. *How can I let her go? She's my mom.* But I allowed myself, for just a moment, to feel that possibility. And I knew in my heart that he was right. It was a difficult moment for me. I'd been affected by my mother's dysregulation my entire life. I'd been thrust into taking on responsibility for her when my father died. Ever since then I'd been trying against the odds to see that she was safe and settled and she was not the least bit interested in cooperating with me in defense of her own wellbeing. It had required a gargantuan amount of effort and determination to get her this far. And now he wanted me to let her go?

A saying in AA invites us to, "Let go and let God." Did I have enough faith in God to do that? Could I trust that the mystical power beyond the limits of this physical reality would look after her? One thing was certain: I couldn't take much more of this. I was at a crossroads.

I wrapped up with Lokpal and went straight to another Zoom call with my women's circle. Halfway through my call, Mom barged into my room. I was right in the middle of sharing my weekly check in.

"Hold on ladies, my mom just came in. Someone else continue." I turned to Mom. "What are you doing? I told you I had a women's call tonight. Thanks for respecting my boundaries. Oh. wait, you've NEVER done that. What do you want?"

"Take me to the train station."

"Fuck! This again? Mother, I am beyond exhausted. It's almost ten o'clock. I am not doing anything tonight. Call a cab if you want to, but I am not doing anything until tomorrow. Just go to sleep." I closed the door and finished up the call, fuming over her lack of consideration. It was the challenge of my life to balance a loving, spiritual way of being in the world with the daily reality of being my mother's daughter. Why did everything have to be so hard?

CHAPTER 27

HAPPY NEW YEAR

December 31, 2015

I woke up the next morning surprised it wasn't brighter outside. I thought I would have slept longer. I turned over and opened my eyes to see Mom was standing over me, fully dressed, holding her umbrella and a yellow duffle bag. A chill ran through my body, and I started shaking. *Does she have a knife? Is she going to kill me?* I was terrified.

"C'mon, let's go," she said. "You're taking me to the train station."

I couldn't believe it. She couldn't let this thing go. A wave of despair washed over me, leaving me feeling totally defeated. *No. No way. I am not giving up.* I got up and got dressed, waves of helplessness alternating with rage.

"Alright, let's go." We drove to the yummy bread place to get breakfast, but I could barely eat for the big lump in my throat and gut. Fighting back tears the entire time, I could not look at her or say anything. We ate in silence and then got in the car.

"Okay," she said. "So, you're taking me to the bus station."

"Yeah, Mom. I'm taking you to the bus station." But I wasn't. I was looking up the address for the Athens police station on Google Maps. I drove straight there.

"This isn't the bus station," she said.

"I know. I'm getting you some maps."

I walked inside and burst into tears.

"Is he hurting you?" the dispatcher behind the counter asked, immediately assuming it was domestic violence.

"It's my mother. She is schizophrenic, she is having an episode, and I don't know what to do."

"Okay, let me find someone for you to talk to."

A moment later the lady shuffled me into an office where a uniformed male officer sat. I shared the whole story of Mom, Dad's passing, her condition, driving down here, and what had happened up until this minute walking into their precinct; I finished by asking for help.

"What are my options?"

A second officer had come in halfway through my story. The two looked at each other. It was the exact same look Dad's lawyers had given me.

"Unless she is a harm to herself or others, there is nothing anyone can do," said one.

"These people have rights," said the other, nodding.

"Really? Really? That's assuming schizophrenics can take care of themselves and make choices. She has no teeth. She is completely blind in her right eye, partially blind in her left eye, and why? Because she refuses to see a doctor, because she thinks the doctor is following her around. She hasn't written a check or been to a grocery store in decades. Does this sound like someone who can take care of themselves, or make rational decisions?"

After I said this, I remembered again how crazy I was to have brought her down here thinking she could live on her own. It was suddenly crystal clear that I had made a horrible mistake. Just like my dad, my desire for Mom to be normal had clouded the truth.

"I agree with you ma'am. It's just that this is the law."

"This law fucking sucks and clearly whoever made it does not understand mental illness. Thanks, politicians. Dumb fucks. So, what are people supposed to do in my situation?" I could feel they felt powerless and wanted to help and I wondered how many times they had seen this scenario? Hiding behind the my-hands-are-tied-let-me-bury-my-head-in-the-sand excuse really didn't work. If more people in law enforcement and community mental health facilities really advocated for these people, I know the laws would change. They would have to. Another example of where the system, failing to treat us as individuals, lets us down with protocol. Why isn't mental health treated on a case-by-case basis? Why does it have to get to a point where people's lives are in danger before anything can be done to help?

They looked down and then back at me with sad, empathetic eyes.

"Well, usually they stay with family members."

"And how am I qualified to take care of a schizophrenic? I am forty, single, and live in a 320-square-foot studio. Not to mention the complex PTSD I have from growing up with the woman. That is not happening. So, basically, no one will do anything. Not until she is homeless and on the streets, babbling to herself, filthy, and God knows what else, before any institution will intervene?"

"Unfortunately, that is the truth. I am sorry. I wish there was something we could do." I just sat there, blinking.

"There is a clinic in town you could check out. A mental health clinic. They might be able to give you some assistance," said the second officer. He pulled out a small notebook, wrote down the name and address, and handed it to me. I accepted it with a glimmer of hope and Googled the address on my phone. It was just down the road, only about ten minutes away. By this time, I had been in the police station for about forty-five minutes. The dispatcher who had ushered me to the office appeared in the doorway.

"Your mother is in the lobby, wondering where you are." I thanked them for their help and went out.

"What are you doing in here?" Mom asked, worried.

"I got you a couple of maps," I replied bitterly.

I handed her the maps I had picked up in the lobby on the way in and we got back in the car. It was now pouring rain and as I pulled out and started driving, I kept adjusting the blower. But the windshield kept fogging up. I couldn't figure it out and my annoyance was growing. *Why does this keep fogging up?* My head was pounding and I could barely see until I realized: I had to use the air conditioner. *What a lame feature.*

"Bus station, bus station," Mom said frantically. "When are we going to the bus station?" It was her mantra this morning. She kept repeating it, over and over and over, and now she was rocking back and forth. I zoomed into the parking lot of Advantage Behavior Health Systems and parked the car.

"This isn't the bus station!" she said.

"I know, Mom. Just wait here. Give me a few minutes."

I walked in and at 8:30 in the morning, it was already a mad house. The waiting room was packed. People were running everywhere, talking to themselves. I stood in a line with a few people in front of me and the conversations I was hearing were fairly hostile. It was clear the receptionist was at the end of her rope from listening to homeless people, addicts, and mental disease patients, day in and day out. Patients talked in frustrated, desperate tones, looking for med refills, expressing physical pain, or dealing with other uncomfortable maladies. The receptionist's responses were all cold and short; she had no patience.

"Go to the room on the left and wait for your name to be called." There were three waiting rooms. Two to the right and one to the left. Each was three quarters full. The employees looked miserable, someplace in between tortured and trapped.

I took one look at the staff members and knew exactly how they felt. Overworked and tired of dealing with all the crazy. I knew that feeling. It takes a toll. I waited until finally it was my turn at the window.

"How can I help you?" It was more of a statement than a question. She was completely shut down, and I knew she was not going to be sympathetic to my case.

"Hi, my name is Heather, and my mother needs help." I explained to her briefly what was happening.

"Go to the room on the right and wait for a counselor. They will call your name." It was a small room with a dozen chairs crammed together, there were seven of us waiting, and not much privacy. I assumed most people were recovering drug addicts because they were all super twitchy and could not sit still. Half had dirty clothes and reeked of body odor. There were no windows, only another receptionist sitting protected behind a wall of glass, holding the power to help or withhold entrance to the clinic door next to her. I found an open seat, sat down, leaned against the wall, closed my eyes in despair, and waited. I didn't have much hope they would actually help Mom, but I had to try, one last time. Every muscle and joint in my body hurt. I desperately just wanted to go home. I kept hearing names called and peeked my eyes open each time. I noticed that people were being called who had come in after me. It had been twenty minutes. Frustrated, I walked up to the window, the same woman sitting there. She glanced up and gave me a look like I was inconveniencing her.

"Hi. I was told I needed to come to this room and my name would be called. It's regarding my mom." She leaned over to look around my body, out into the waiting room.

"Where is your mother?"

"She's out in the car. She won't come in, but she is having a schizophrenic episode and needs help."

The woman looked at me and blinked, like she couldn't believe I could be so stupid. "If she won't come in," she said slowly, "there is nothing we can do."

I stood there, utterly stunned. I stared at the woman without seeing her. I felt as though I was no longer there, but watching as some kind of observer, just watching everything transpire before me. My thoughts were hollow. *I can't believe this. My life has become total insanity. No one gives a shit about Mom, or me, or what is happening. It's like I'm just trying to buy a bottle of water and the store is all out. 'Oh well. Try next time.'*

I turned and walked out. Walked out of all the crazy. Walked out of everything. *That's it, I am done. There is nothing more I can do.*

I got back in the car shocked and numb. Mom's mantra had ramped up to a fever pitch and volume. She was now rocking and screaming, "take me to the bus, take me to the bus, take me to the bus," over and over and over, her eyes glassy and staring. I looked up Greyhound on my phone, started the car, and gunned it, tires squealing to get me across to the far-right lane; I drove like a bat out of hell. My jaws hurt and my ears roared.

"SHUT UP, Rain Man!" I growled through my teeth. "We are going there now! Just shut up." I swerved, passing people left and right.

I was expecting a large Greyhound station, but it was just a small gas station with a Greyhound sign and a bench. We went inside and I started crying again.

"Where do you want to go, Momma?"

"Memphis."

"One ticket to Memphis, please," I said to the man, tears streaming down my face. He handed me the ticket. The bus wasn't leaving for another hour.

"The bus leaves at 10:50 a.m., Mom, and you won't get in until 11 o'clock tonight. You will have a long layover in Atlanta."

"Okay. That's fine." We had an hour to kill.

"There is a Barnes and Noble we passed on the way, just down the road. Do you want to go there and walk around?"

"Yeh, that's fine."

Big drops of cold rain began falling from gray clouds as I walked into Barnes and Noble, Mom a few steps behind me. A flood of grief and terror suddenly struck me, my mind heavy like I was under water. I became so dizzy and nauseated I had to grab onto a bookshelf. My vision started going in and out as well. I tried to focus on a magazine cover, but the whole room was spinning. I moved down the aisle, past the magazines, into travel books. *Maybe I can distract myself.* But that wasn't happening; it only made everything worse. Mom was two steps behind. I glanced at her, hoping she would pick up a book or something. But her eyes, wide and vacant, were locked on me. Swallowing hard and fighting back the urge to wretch, I turned and hurried to the door, emerging back out into a torrential rainfall, and climbing into the driver's seat. Mom climbed into the passenger seat. We were both soaking wet and my hands and body were shaking. I had nothing to say to her. Through the roar in my ears, I heard Lokpal's soothing voice, telling me I needed to let her go.

Will I ever see her again after today? If this was the last moment, what do I say? I had nothing. My heart was overworked, shut down, and crucified by this human sitting next to me. I had nothing.

It was now almost a quarter to eleven. I started the car and we drove back. The bus was already there. I walked Mom to the bus. She was clutching her ticket in one hand, her duffle bag and the umbrella in the other. It was gentle steady rain, now. She stood behind me, still expecting me to take the lead.

"Hand him your ticket, Mom."

"Oh. Here you go." The man took the ticket. I gave Mom a quick hug as she patted me on the back, her eyes still vacant.

"Bye, Momma. Hope you get there safe. You have enough money?"

"Yeh, I got money."

"Okay." I got back in the car and watched her silhouette move to the back of the bus. Wearing her visor, umbrella in one hand, yellow duffle bag in the other. She sat down, not seeing me. And as the bus pulled away, I cried harder than I have ever cried in my life. I could not catch my breath and I was choking on phlegm and saliva. *Will I ever see her again?* This was the first time in forty-two years she had done anything on her own. Would she get beaten, raped, mugged?

I pulled out my phone and dialed my friend Lesa. I couldn't talk. She listened to me cry.

"Oh my gosh, baby, what's wrong. Baby, what's wrong?" I couldn't say a word.

"Do you want me to pray for you?"

"Yes," is all I could get out.

"Do you want me to have Aravel pray, too?" Aravel was another one of our friends.

"Yeah."

"Okay, we'll do it right now."

"I'll call you later to check in." I couldn't drive. I was crying uncontrollably for what seemed like hours, experiencing the grief while simultaneously disassociated and what felt like an altered state of consciousness. It was still raining; the heavens were crying with me.

*   *   *

After a while I could finally make my way back to the apartment. I felt like a ghost. Every part of me had been ripped apart and there was nothing left of me. I called the police in Memphis, Tennessee, and explained to them what was happening. I asked if someone could please go to the bus station at eleven o'clock tonight and check on Mom. The lady was really nice.

"We don't usually do things like that but if you call back an hour before, I will send someone over."

"Oh, thank you so much, okay. I'll call back."

I moved Mom's bed into my room and laid down for a while. When I woke up, I canceled the flight reservation I had made the day before. I had to figure out what to do with this apartment and all of Mom's stuff. I had no idea what was going to happen, but I began rifling through all the boxes and bags to find things I would want or need. Photo albums, year books, Mom's social security card, all the death and birth certificates, and to my astonishment, there it was: Mom and Dad's marriage license that I had fought so hard to get a copy of. I could not find the bag that was supposed to have Dad's clothes in it that Mom was going to use to make a quilt. If she didn't make it, I was going to have someone else do it. But it wasn't there. I did find some of his winter stuff, some wool socks and Under Armour long underwear. I stuffed those in my suitcase.

I went to the grocery store and got what I thought would be benign food: salads and fruit. But the dressing made me sick, and I threw it all away.

I packed my suitcase with my clothes, Christmas gifts, and all the things I found that I wanted to bring home. I pulled up some music by Australian singer/songwriter Vance Joy on my computer and danced around my room a bit, trying to get back in my body. I drew a bath and sat in stillness. The night sky outside was full of fireworks. It was New Year's Eve, 2015. *What a way to spend New Year's. I am alone in a strange place; Mom is God knows where. Sure doesn't feel like New Year's.* I crawled into bed at ten o'clock, barely able to keep my eyes open, and called Memphis Police again. The same lady answered the phone.

"Hi, ma'am, this is Heather. I called earlier about my mom."

"Hi there. I'll send someone over. What's your number? They will call you when they get there."

"Great." I gave her my number. "Thanks so much for your help. Happy New Year."

"Happy New Year to you also."

We disconnected and I fell asleep. I woke up to my phone ringing with a Memphis number. It was just past one in the morning.

"Hello, this is Heather."

"Hi. This is Officer Brown. Your mom is here at the bus station and she is fine. She's wanting to go to Oxford, but there isn't a bus that goes to Oxford. She would have to go to Tupelo. That bus comes at six thirty in the morning. She would have to stay the night in the bus station."

"Okay, well that is great news. Thank you so much for calling and going out of your way to help me. I know this isn't protocol. Happy New Year to you, sir."

"And you too, ma'am. Glad we can help and that your mom is okay. If there is anything else you need, just give us a call. Goodbye now."

"Goodbye."

Mom survived a twelve-hour bus ride, safe and sound, totally intact, and now she wanted to go home to Oxford. That was the best news I'd heard in a long time. My prayers had been answered. My body released weeks of tension, and I felt gratitude to the bed for supporting me. *Maybe this is finally over.* I quickly drifted back to sleep.

It was still dark when the phone rang again. Five o'clock. I jolted out of sleep and saw that it was a Memphis number again. I knew it was Mom.

"Hello?" I said.

"Yeh, it's me. Will you come get me? I had to stay the night in the bus station. I'm trying to get to Oxford but there's no bus."

"Yes, I'll come get you."

"Okay, bye."

"Wait, Mom, wait…Mom!" *Shit, she didn't wait for me to tell her when I would be there!* I quickly looked at the GPS. It's a seven-and-a-half-hour drive from Athens to Memphis. *Fuck.* I leaped up, got dressed, grabbed my suitcase, the bags I'd packed the previous night, the computer I bought Mom for Christmas, and threw everything the car. I paused for a long while and stood outside the front door of the apartment, looking at all of Mom and Dad's stuff. Their whole life was there in bags and chaos in every room. *Should I take the keys, or leave them?* I had no idea what we were going to do, but I didn't feel that we would ever come back here. I left the keys on the TV stand and shut the door.

I had to stop and get gas. I was so freaked out, the world was spinning dizzily around me. I sat in the car and looked at the GPS. *Is there a faster way? Did I type in the right address?* Seven-and-a-half hours, was it? I started to drive away and heard a big noise next to the car like I'd hit something and jammed on the brakes. *You've got to be kidding me, what the fuck was that?*

When I opened the door, I saw the gas nozzle lying on the ground. I'd driven off with it still in the car. I've never done that in my life; I have never even forgotten to put the gas cap on. *Wow, I am totally losing it. Am I even fit to drive?* Exhausted couldn't even begin to describe how I felt. It was like I was living someone else's life. Every part of me was depleted. I pictured those marathon runners at the end of a race, with their knees caving in as they pissed themselves, and crawled across the finish line.

I took off. I drove one hundred miles an hour almost the whole way there, with the exception of the drive through Atlanta, where there was traffic. Somewhere in Alabama I saw a Greyhound bus drive by in the opposite direction. *Is Mom on that bus? Did she change her mind? Was she going back to Athens?* I kept driving like a mad woman and got to the Memphis bus station at 12:30 p.m., two hours ahead of schedule.

The terminal was huge. From the outside it looked like an old airline hangar. I ran inside and quickly skimmed the area, looking for Mom's navy-blue visor. I didn't see Mom anywhere. *Okay, the bathroom.* I dashed into the ladies' room and looked under each stall for Mom's feet in their blue Keds. I looked in the café. I walked around the entire building three times. No Mom. I walked the perimeter. In the back were a dozen parked buses. I looked under and around each one of them. I know this sounds excessive, but Mom was unpredictable.

I searched Days Creek. Did she fall in, drown, or kill herself? I didn't see any floating bodies. On the east side of the station, on the opposite side of the street, I spied a string of greasy-spoon fast-food restaurants. I ran in, disheveled and frantic, scanning for Mom, but didn't see her. By the third restaurant, tears started flowing.

"Mom, where the fuck are you?" I yelled. "Why didn't you wait for me?" Mental and emotional paralysis was setting in again and my brain went on autopilot. I slowly walked back to the station, keeping my eyes open for a bright yellow duffle bag. Once inside, I went to the ticket counter. Three women talked amongst themselves behind the glass, oblivious to my presence. I listened as they gossiped about their love lives and lady parts. *Really? Could you be any more inappropriate?* I stood there for what seemed like forever before they even looked at me.

"Can I help you?" said one, in a clipped, passive-aggressive tone, seemingly annoyed by my intrusion.

"Hi. I'm looking for my mom. She is five-foot-two, one hundred and forty pounds, wearing a navy-blue visor, blue sweatpants and T-shirt, and blue Keds shoes and she's carrying a yellow duffle bag and an umbrella. She arrived here last night from Athens and was waiting to take a bus to Tupelo this morning. But then she called me at 5:00 a.m. to come get her. Have you seen her?" The woman seemed irritated by my request.

"Well, we don't allow people to stay the night. What's your mom's name? I'll look her up to see if she bought a bus ticket."

"Her name is Susan Moore."

"I don't see her name here, maybe she went to a hotel." I know for a fact she would not have gone to a hotel.

"She called me from this number." I showed her the number on my cell phone.

"That's not a number we have here." *Bullshit.* Meanwhile the other two hadn't stopped their conversation among themselves. I was blown away by how rude they were. *I'm missing my mother, you assholes! Pay attention!*

One of them finally noticed me.

"You can file a missing person's report," she suggested. It seemed drastic. I thought I'd wait a while to see if she turned up. Maybe she went for a walk.

I called the number Mom had called me from and I could hear a phone ringing, but I couldn't tell where it was coming from. I walked to the adjacent offices next to the ticket line, but it seemed like it was getting farther away. After five rings it would stop. I walked back to the café and called again. I could hear it in the background, but it was coming from somewhere else. After three more attempts I figured out it was coming from a pay phone in the middle of the terminal.

Okay, at least I know she did call from here. I walked the terminal inside and out two more times. Still no Mom. It was now 1:30 a.m. and I'd been searching for her for thirteen hours. I called Memphis Police to file a missing person's report.

"Okay, we'll send someone over shortly." I waited and waited, sitting in the car for a while, then getting up and walking around. I vacillated between being bored out of my mind and running worst-case scenarios in my head. I kept checking the time. It was nearing three o'clock. *Clearly my case was not a priority.*

As I was walking back inside to go to the bathroom a fight broke out right inside the doorway. A woman was causing a problem, and one of the women who I had overheard talking about her vagina at the ticket window was trying to eject her from the building. Punches and bodies were being thrown against the glass so hard I thought it would break. I'd never seen a fight before. It seemed an appropriate demonstration of what had been going on inside of me over the previous two weeks. I decided to walk down to another entrance. When I came out of the bathroom the police were there, breaking up the fight.

I stood to the side, waiting for the officer to finish his report, and then approached him.

"I called hours ago to file a missing person's report. Can you help me?" He seemed distracted and didn't look too enthused at my question. *Maybe he's dating one of the ticket window ladies?* Officer Robert Shannon pointed to a small kiosk close to the door, and we walked over together. I gave him Mom's name and driver's license number, and a good description of her, and he typed it all into a small laptop. As I was answering his questions, his phone beeped constantly with text messages. I glanced down and could see they were all from the same person, probably his girlfriend, judging from the smile on his face. *What is it with people down here? Their personal lives seem a lot more important than their jobs.*

After we finished writing up the report, he and his partner drove off to check the hotels. I wasn't hopeful. When they came back an hour later with an empty car I was not surprised.

"The report will be filed tonight. Call us if she turns up." *Wow.* I couldn't believe their lack of concern.

I wasn't sticking around Memphis, and I wasn't going back to Athens either, so I called Uncle Ed.

CHAPTER 28

UNCLE ED'S

Uncle Ed was in New Orleans when I reached him and since there was no point in beating about the bush, I gave him the straight goods.

"Mom got on a bus, and I was supposed to pick her up in Memphis, but she isn't here. I filed a police report."

"What did she go to Memphis for?"

"I have no idea. She's gone off the deep end and I need to rest. Can I go to your house?"

"Of course, you can go to the house. I'll see you there tomorrow."

"Okay, Uncle. Love you." I drove to Oxford, an hour-and-a-half from Memphis.

On the drive Lokpal's voice whispered from deep within, *you need to let your mom go.* I felt complete, totally resolved. I knew I had done absolutely everything in my power to help her. What happened after today was in God's hands. With a deep exhale, I let her go. In that moment I was ok if I never saw her again, every part of me complete. I released the both of us.

As soon as I got to Uncle's house, I took a shower. Finally, a place I felt comfortable. I'd spent a week here a couple of years earlier. The familiarity brought safety and a sense of ease. I knew the bed, refrigerator, TV, laundry. I knew what kind of food would be there, where the nearest coffee shop was. I was struck by how knowing a place can bring such grounding and relief to a stressed out body.

I needed to go home, so I bought a ticket for January 3. I had to go. I just couldn't worry about Mom anymore. Wherever she was, God would take care of her, even if that meant she was homeless. I zoned out on *Law and Order*.

When the phone rang with a Memphis number, I immediately thought that Mom must be dead.

"Hello, this is Heather."

"Hello ma'am this is Sergeant Williams. Just calling to see how you are and if you heard from your mom."

His voice was full of sweetness and concern. Like a friend coming to pick me up and hug me.

"Hello Sergeant. Thank you so much for calling. No, I haven't heard from her yet. I will let you know if I do. You haven't heard anything?"

"No ma'am, but we have our eyes and ears open for her. Okay ma'am, I will check in with you soon."

I went to bed continuing to pray and continuing to give it over to God. When I woke up, I was excited at the prospect of spending the day in Oxford and catching up with Uncle Ed when he got home. I drove to Best Buy in Tupelo to return the computer I had bought for Mom for Christmas, since I thought she wouldn't be using it anytime soon. Oxford being home to Ole Miss—the University of Mississippi—you'd think they would have a Best Buy, but they don't. I was halfway there when Uncle Ed called.

"Hey, your mother called and left a message on the landline. I couldn't understand what she said, but I think she's at a hotel."

"Holy shit! Okay, well I'm returning her computer in Tupelo, so I'll call you when I get back."

"Okay, bye." *Damn, I'm forty-five minutes away. She better not run off again.* I returned the computer and raced like hell to get back. When I pulled into Uncle Ed's driveway, his good friend Martha was there moving the garbage cans. *Oh crap. This woman talks non-stop, and you can never understand a word she says.* I flung open the car door and ran inside past her.

"Hey, Martha!"

"Hey, Heather! I didn't know you'd be here. I was looking for that key earlier."

"Sorry, Martha. I'm in a hurry right now, I can't talk to you." She continued talking but I ran for the phone. I didn't listen to the voicemail, I just looked at caller ID, saw Motel 8, and pressed "call back."

"Hello, Motel 8."

"Hi, my name is Heather and I'm looking for my mom. She's white, 5'2", and she's wearing blue sweatpants, a shirt, and a navy-blue visor; she's carrying a yellow duffle bag, and she's schizophrenic. I think she's staying with you."

"There is a woman sitting in the lobby that fits that description."

"Oh my God, really? Will you tell her I'm coming to get her?"

"Are you sure you want me to do that?" the lady said. "She might run off."

"Oh. That's a good idea. Where are you? Are you in Memphis?"

"No, we're in Oxford." *Holy shit!*

"I'll be right there." I ran back to the car and followed the GPS to the motel. I pulled up right outside the front door, flung the car door open, and I could see Mom sitting there. The hotel's automatic doors opened, and I started sobbing.

"Momma, where have you been? I have been looking everywhere for you."

"What are you doing here? I was waiting for Ed." Mom started crying and we grabbed each other. She was soaking wet and shivering.

"Why are you wet?"

"I washed my clothes in the tub." I grabbed her things and started to walk out. I turned to the receptionist. She had her hand over her mouth, tears streaming down her face. I mouthed "thank you" and she nodded her head. She was my angel that day. Another moment I will never forget.

"Momma, Ed is in New Orleans for New Year's. He'll be back today. Why didn't you wait for me in Memphis? How did you get here?"

"I took a bus to Tupelo and then a cab. Something is really wrong with me. I don't feel well at all. Something is really wrong. I'm so tired, my mind isn't right. I don't think I can take care of myself."

"Do you want to go to the hospital?"

"Yeah, I think I need to go. I don't feel right, something is really wrong with me. I don't feel good at all."

This was the moment I had been waiting for my whole life. I could take her to the hospital right now, and she would voluntarily admit herself. But I didn't. I froze with fear. I didn't want to do it by myself. I wanted to wait for Uncle Ed, and I also wanted to get Mom out of her wet clothes. She looked awful. Like she had been chewed up and spit out a few times over. Her face was a shade of pale green, and she looked exhausted.

"Let's go to Uncle Ed's and you can take a shower."

"How can we go to Ed's if he isn't there?"

"I called him yesterday and stayed there last night, spare key."

Back at Uncle Ed's, I showed Mom around the house, and she perked up a bit. She was excited to be looking at family photos, pictures from all the years she had missed.

"Oh, here is Uncle Ron, and David and Ed." She picked up the frame and rubbed her hand over it, gazing at it for a while. I wondered what she was thinking. She continued to look around the rest of the house, her hands behind her back, pacing. She was studying, scrutinizing every detail.

"Yeh, this is Ed's house," she finally said. "Well, I'll be." I sighed, irritated that she still thought I might be lying to her.

"Mom, why don't you take a shower. I'll put your clothes in the wash."

"Where's the washer and dryer?"

"It's outside in the small garage under the carport. Do you have something else to wear?"

"No, not really."

"I brought some of your clothes. There, in that bag in the guest room."

While Mom took a shower, I put her clothes in the wash. I was relieved but I also didn't want to take my eyes off her for fear she would wander off. After her shower she took a nap. It was around four o'clock, Uncle Ed would be home in a couple of hours. I found *Law and Order* on TV and zoned out for a while.

A friend of mine was doing a meditation online at five thirty. I logged on and listened until I heard Uncle Ed walk through the door. I got up and peeked through the crack of the bedroom door which had a sightline to the living room. I expected Uncle Ed to embrace my mother. After all, he had not seen his sister in thirty-eight years. But what I saw was anger and concern on his face, and there was no embrace.

"Hello, Ed," Mom said with a big grin, clearly happy to see him.

"Hello, Susan." He walked past her. I walked out and gave him a hug.

"Welcome home, Uncle. How was your holiday?"

"Oh, it was fine." We sat down and started talking, and he showed Mom some pictures.

"Where did you find your mother?"

"She was at Motel 8 down the street."

"Susan, why did you want to go to Athens?"

"I don't know, online it said it was a good place to retire."

"Martha and Mellissa went to school there. They lived there for eight years." We continued talking for thirty minutes or so. When I went out to smoke, Uncle Ed followed.

"So, what are you going to do with your mom?"

"Uncle, I'm so sorry to do this to you, but I'm going home tomorrow. I bought my ticket last night. I had no idea if I was going to see Mom again. I've been gone nearly three weeks, and I've hardly eaten or slept. I am exhausted and I have nothing left to give anyone. I'm leaving her with you. I can come back in a month or so to help you find her a place, but I need a break. I need space away from her. I can't breathe."

I could see he wasn't happy about it, but he agreed. When we got back inside, Uncle Ed asked us more questions. When had we left Detroit? How much money did Mom have? What was her social security, her pension? I told him all about my estate disaster, and the whole story of moving, going to Memphis, and now coming here. He was pissed.

"Susan, do you know how much you have put Heather through? You are really selfish. Do you see how selfish you are?" I was stunned. No one had ever defended me against my mother before. Dad certainly never did. But here was my uncle, taking my side, protecting me. It felt *so … damn … good*.

"Yeh, well I'm not right in the head. What do you want me to do?"

"Well, you've got to grow up at some point." He continued to share how angry he was all these years that she had never responded to anyone's phone calls or letters, not even when Mam'maw or Papaw died. I was so impressed. He laid out all his feelings and really let her have it. Dad had always been too soft on her. Perhaps he was just beaten down and defeated after living with her so long, and he'd had nothing left to fight with.

After family confession, it was time for dinner. Uncle Ed only eats meat and occasionally has a vegetable on the side.

"Call Abner's and order some chicken. I'll go pick it up." Abner's is a famous chicken joint in Oxford.

As we were eating, I watched Mom and her brother, reunited after thirty-eight years. The talk earlier had released a lot of buried emotion and hurt, and now we were left with just us. I watched as Mom and Ed bantered, laughed, bickered. I was surprised at how similar Ed's personality was to Dad's. They were only a week apart in age. Maybe that had something to do with it.

I was grateful to be witness to this moment. I don't know what it's like to have a sibling, but I could feel some joy bubbling up in Ed as his sister stood in front of him, flesh and blood. Mom, not having teeth, had to cut her chicken into little bits and gnash at it. The sound was so irritating. I was laughing at Ed making fun of Mom. He kept jabbing her with little insults that were sarcastic but filled with truth and love. He was trying to see how far he could go with her. Mom was pretty defenseless, but he didn't care.

After dinner I set up the pullout couch and lay down. Uncle Ed went to watch TV in his room and Mom went to bed in the guest room where I'd slept the night before. The thought of going home in the morning was blissful. My body started to relax at a deeper level. I knew that Mom would be safe here and I didn't have to worry about her anymore. Uncle Ed was here and hopefully Uncle Ronnie would also be getting involved.

We all slept until nine o'clock the next morning. After coffee I finished packing and loaded up the car. I was supposed to have returned it days ago in Athens and was nervous about returning it in Memphis. I hadn't called the car rental to let them know my plans.

Mom still looked like crap and Uncle Ed had a concerned, deer-in-the-headlights kind of look. *They'll figure it out.*

"Okay, y'all. I'm taking off." We were out on the front lawn. I hugged both of them, said I would call when I got home, and drove away.

Oh Lord, finally I have some freedom and peace.

Spending these weeks with Mom 24/7 had left me in pieces, beyond recognition. I was going to schedule some acupuncture, a chiropractor appointment, a massage, a haircut, and a hot springs visit for the following week. When I arrived at the Memphis Enterprise office, no one questioned how long I'd had the car or why I was suddenly nine hundred miles away from where I was supposed to drop it off. *Thank God,* I thought, and proceeded to the departures area of the airport. I walked the long corridor riddled with Elvis sculptures and paraphernalia to the United Airlines check in. My suitcase weighed in at fifty-four pounds.

"You can only have fifty pounds. You can either take stuff out or pay $100." *This is a scam. You limit bags to fifty pounds so your workers don't get injured, but if I pay you $100 you still take my bag and your employee still gets injured?*

I took out my high school yearbooks—they weighed five pounds each. Why they made these things so big is beyond me, they could practically survive a nuclear blast. Now I had my hands full. A carry-on, my purse, ten pounds of yearbooks and a twelve-inch-wide stone sundial Mom had given me years ago that I'd never taken back to California. I ended up cracking the tip off in the airport bathroom. *Urgh, I can't get a break.*

During the flight I sat and had no thoughts. There was nothing to do except to sit and let go. I stared out the window and slept. The stress was finally gone, and I could take my armor off. I had just been through a war, an internal war of impatience, control, rage, fear, loss and abandonment. I felt like I'd been shot through a canon and had exploded inside. I had forgotten all of what I'd learned through my years of spiritual practice— all the tools I knew to use to be present. All of them. I'd been thrown into the deep end of a toxic pool and I flailed about. I was disappointed in myself, how I had reacted to and treated Mom. I'd been full of just too much fear, hurt, and resentment. It had consumed me.

On the layover in Houston, I sat gazing at the gate sign in red that said, "SAN FRANCISCO 6:45 P.M." I reflected on all of my experiences while living in the Bay Area. I was so excited to be going home, feeling that it *was* my home, and wondering why I had spent the last six months trying to leave. Since my failed trip to Denver, I'd begun looking through a different lens and I saw how blessed I was, saw the opportunities, the lifestyle I had at my fingertips. I thought, *contentment really is a state of mind that involves transforming all your past. In certain ways you have to rewrite experience to create meaning and empower the Self.* My internal perspective shifted off center from where it habitually was and the teaching clicked into place. That growing up and maturing into soul wisdom is the process of taking radical responsibility for my internal being and experience.

When I am under severe stress, I don't eat. My traveling diet of late had consisted of Diet Coke, coffee, and cigarettes. Once the stress subsides, I end up with horrible diarrhea. I had been to the bathroom twice already, carrying all my bags. After the second time, I came and sat down and immediately had to go again. After my third bathroom incident I called my friend Lizzy.

"Hey, girl." Hearing her voice, I started to cry again.

"Hey Chica, how are you?" I didn't talk to her much about my trip because she was with family from Wisconsin, but I gave her a brief synopsis. "I'm just soooo ready to come home, and I need to get laid." What I desperately needed was relief: kindness, softness, pleasure, sensuality so I could forget the chaos of my mind and the last six months and get back in my body.

"Do you have any prospects?"

"Yeah, auto body guy. It's moving so slow, though. I don't know if he's into me."

"Who could not be into you? He would be an idiot." We both laughed.

"Alright love, I'm about to board. I'll see you at ten thirty at the airporter. Can't wait to see you. Love you."

"Love you, babes."

CHAPTER 29

RESPITE: BACK HOME

January 4, 2015

Chris and I had started hanging out after I got into a small car accident in my driveway that required bodywork. He wanted to try acupuncture, so we did a trade as payment. We had dinner or lunch many times, but he never made a move.

Since getting sober, I wondered whether I had lost my touch. I was so used to having sex on the first, second, or third date. *Do I need to be inebriated to attract a man?* My last long-term relationship had taken place six years earlier. I knew I wasn't a spring chicken, and the reality of age was hitting me sideways. Just one more thing to add to my current bag of horrors. Truth to tell, after the nightmare of the previous year, it was a relief to have stable male energy in my life again.

When I got home to my studio in the woods, I was instantly grounded. Safe and held in the womb of the familiar. I knew what to expect here, I knew how to navigate the energy, and, most meaningfully, Mom wasn't here.

I spent the next week sleeping and barely left my house, except for all my self-care appointments. I had a couple of light days in the office but nothing overwhelming. I had to deal with breaking the lease in Athens. They required the missing person's report, and they also wanted a doctor's note for Mom. *How the hell am I going to get a doctor's note? I can't get this woman to go to the doctor.*

Weeks later I went to Minneapolis to visit a friend. While I was there my realtor and my attorneys called me every day to sign off on repairs for two of the houses my dad had owned and, also, to start the process of signing the closing documents for the sales. I also had to start the eviction process on the third property, whose tenants had not paid rent in six months. To add to my vacation-turned-work experience, before I had left Mississippi, my mom, her brothers, and I had decided to donate all of Mom's belongings in the Athens apartment to Habitat for Humanity. It would have cost $2,000 for movers to move it all from Athens to Oxford, plus storage costs, so we decided it wasn't worth the hassle. We could get Mom new stuff. Habitat for Humanity needed a written letter from me saying that it could all be donated, and to give them permission to enter the apartment. I got a call two days later saying they needed another letter because they hadn't been able to take everything in one day.

I was so agitated by all the little laws and rules one has to abide by that in my mind were a complete waste of my time. Everything must be in writing and all of it documented. I was tired of signing, notarizing, and giving permission for every little thing that I or someone else needed to do. I wanted to say, "Just do it for Christ's sake!"

Chris picked me up from the Airporter when I got home from Minneapolis. At this point, I had given up on the possibility of us having a relationship and resigned our status to "good friends." We stopped in Fairfax for dinner at a Thai place and talked about my trip. It catalyzed us into sharing our past relationship experiences and we spoke candidly about our issues and shortcomings. I felt safe with him. His honesty and vulnerability amazed me because it was so natural for him. He was a *real* man. I had read about them in books but had never met one in the flesh and my inner feminine was squealing with excitement to have a grounded masculine presence in my life. I was really wanting someone else to take the lead, I was tired of making all the decisions. We walked back to his autobody shop, and he opened the vertical door. I stood poised to give him a goodbye hug, as I'd done many times before, and then he kissed me. Finally, the moment I had been waiting for months for! I liked it. Slow, soft, big lips. My defenses dropped, vulnerability emerged, and I let myself be held. *I can stand with this man and he can hold me up. He will protect me, take care of me, he isn't afraid of my emotions, and I can see they actually soften his heart and demeanor. This is real.*

I knew in that moment that Dad had brought this person into my life, even if it was for a short time, to give me some companionship and lighten my burden. Our final conversation flashed in my memory. Dad had been worried about me being alone, and I had told him I wanted a man's man, someone just like him. And now, that man was standing in front of me. I had resisted dating when a mutual friend had first told me about Chris. But then, after damaging my car, in my own driveway of all places, I was forced to go meet this guy. It was just too perfect.

We kissed a while longer and had a long embrace. I loved his huge arms and his broad chest. He was so snuggly, like a bear. I loved it.

The next few weeks allowed me to settle into a good routine. Accounts were open, bills were getting paid, houses were being fixed and sold, and it all required less of my attention. I could finally start to grieve Dad. I would sit in front of my altar every day and do my morning sadhana—a spiritual ritual—and my heart would open a little more, day by day. Tears would flow and my heart would ache.

*   *   *

Mid-February 2016

After a typical Saturday in the office, I went to Chris's house in Petaluma. We had planned a day of riding the motorcycle and playing in bed. I walked up to the door, and it flung open: Chris was there greeting me with a huge grin and a hug. My phone started ringing.

"Shit, it's Uncle Ed." I paused for a moment wondering if I should answer it or not. "Hi Uncle Ed."

"Hi. So, we have to talk about your mother. Ron and Savina are on the line too." My heart sank and started to race. I knew this was not going to be a good conversation. "Okay, what's going on?"

"I have tried for weeks now to get your mother to go look at apartments and houses. I've been busting my ass to find something for her and she won't go look at anything. She is not my responsibility. I am fed up with her. Now I'm leaving in a couple of weeks to go on vacation and I do not want her to stay here while I'm gone. Ron and Savina don't want her, either."

"I know. She has been like this my whole life. This is nothing new." The three of them cut me off, all jumping in at once:

"There's something wrong with her."

"She's not our responsibility."

"You have to come and get her."

I started tuning them out as my rage started to surface. It busted out like a superhero, screaming. "Are you kidding me?

You've had her for one month and you are beside yourselves? I've lived with this my whole life. I cannot do this next step by myself. Ed, you are an attorney, Ron, you are a doctor. We aren't stupid people. I'm telling you right now I AM NOT BRINGING HER TO CALIFORNIA, it is out of the question, so stop asking me. I have asked for your help many times and you have brushed me off. YOU are her family also, not just me. I don't care what we have to do, but she needs to be put in a mental hospital. I looked into doing it in Michigan, but it wasn't going to get approved. So, why don't you for the first time in YOUR life, show up for your sister."

There was a long pause. I couldn't believe what I had just said, to people I didn't even really know. But it needed to be said.

Finally, Uncle Ed broke the silence. "Okay, let's put her in the hospital. I gotta tell you though that here in Mississippi she will have to sit in jail until there is a bed available."

"I don't care, Uncle, do what you have to do, just get it done."

"Okay. I'll file the paperwork on Monday." We hung up. I was trembling. Chris could hear me yelling from the bedroom. When I walked out he grabbed me, stroked my hair, and held me for a long time.

Uncle Ed, being who he is, walked straight into the Oxford Court House and got his judge friend to sign involuntary committal documents for Mom. It was finalized on February 24, 2016. Uncle Ed was leaving in a couple of days for his trip. Two huge 6'2" US Marshalls came to the house. When they arrived, Mom was in her room.

"Susan, there is someone here to see you," Uncle Ed said. When Mom came out, they handcuffed her and put her in the back of a police car. Uncle Ed had told her all of this beforehand so she would know what to expect but she hadn't believed him.

Mom had taken her purse to the jail with her, and they confiscated it when she arrived. Uncle Ed received a call from an officer there saying that Mom had $5,000 in her purse, did he want to come get it? Uncle Ed swiftly went down to pick it up and put it in a bank account for her. She told me she had money when we were traveling together but I never thought she would be carrying that much. It's a miracle it didn't get stolen or lost.

I didn't talk to Mom until she was in North Mississippi State Hospital in Tupelo a few days later. Uncle Ed told me to call her because the patients couldn't call out during their first week there.

When I called the receptionist checked to see if I was on the "call" list before putting me through.

"Hello?" Mom actually sounded pretty good.

"Hi Momma. How's it going, what's it been like?"

"Oh, I'm okay. Well, I spent a day and a night in a holding cell, with no food, waiting for all my paperwork to go through. I cried a lot and stood at the bars and yelled 'I don't belong in here, I need a preacher,' over and over." We laughed.

"Why were you yelling for a preacher? What was he going to do for you?"

"I don't know; I haven't been in my right mind for years. Guess I thought he could help me."

"What did the guards say?"

"They said, 'there is no preacher here ma'am, you sit down and stop your yelling'." I laughed again.

"Oh my, Mom, that's funny and terrible."

"Then they transferred me to county jail for two days. I wore a green jumpsuit and sat in a cell by myself. You couldn't leave. People were just talking all night long. I hadn't slept in days. Then a female police officer came and got me and brought me to the hospital. They have a whole team of people here, psychiatrists, psychologists, nurses. I had to sit in front of all of them and answer questions. They gave me a test where the doctor listed things like apple, water, and wind, and asked me to recite them back, and I couldn't. But I'm good with numbers. I can do math and such on paper. They said I have short term memory loss. I asked them is it dementia and they said no, it's like dementia but not dementia. They really focus on nutrition and the food is good, it's balanced. We get a vegetable, a meat, fruit, and dairy. When I first got here in the mornings I was real dizzy and didn't feel good. They gave me some juice and snacks and discovered I have hypoglycemia too. It's helped my energy. I don't feel so tired and out of it. My brain feels like it works. They also diagnosed me with disorganized schizophrenia, so now I'm taking a medication called Geodon. I'm the oldest one in here. There's a girl who calls me granny." We both laughed. "And we have group therapy every day, go outside for an hour. It's okay. I guess it could be worse."

"Good, Momma, I'm glad you're finally getting the help you need."

"Yeh, me too. Well, I gotta go, they only give you ten minutes. Can you call Ronnie and ask him to call me?"

"Sure, Momma. Talk later, love you."

"I love you."

I was mortified at what Mom had gone through. This is how we treat mentally ill people? I was so grateful that Mom was getting the help she desperately needed, but for her to be treated like a criminal was heartbreaking and baffling.

Uncle Ed returned from his trip, and we started discussing what to do with Mom when she got out. There was a possibility of her getting released before thirty days, and he wasn't happy about that. He wanted her to stay in as long as possible. He was gun shy and afraid he would have to be exposed to more of her craziness. I told him she would be different now that she was on meds. He wasn't convinced. Which I understand. It's hard being around someone who is mentally ill. It's draining and scary. I told him I would come out and find her a place. Easter was on March 27 which Mom spent in the hospital; I arrived on the 29th.

Mom looked really good. She had lost some weight, and we talked at length about her journey in the hospital and what she had learned about her disease. For the first time in my life, a part of her seemed at peace. Like a starving child who needed food and had finally got fed. Prior to her release, she was mandated by the court to go to a mental health clinic in Oxford once a month for a check in and to renew her prescription. I was so relieved that she was finally in the "system," meaning that government bodies knew about her. I always feared that if something happened to her there would be no record to prove her existence.

The day after I arrived it was house hunting time. Ed's good friend Martha had been researching places for rent over the previous couple of weeks preparing for Mom's return. We took two cars. Ed and Martha in one, and Mom, Ronnie, Savina, and me in another. Based on our last phone conversation I wasn't sure how the dynamic was going to be, but everyone seemed very calm. It turned out that Savina's good friend from medical school (in Bulgaria!) was Mom's doctor in the hospital. Savina, Ronnie, and the doctors at the hospital had been in close communication while Mom was staying there; all parties were very pleased with how far Mom had come.

Fortunately, it didn't take long for us to find the place Mom wanted—a two-bedroom, two-bathroom house. It was right around the corner from Ed's house in a new subdivision. We looked at it and an hour later we were signing the lease, although Mom couldn't move in until April 24th. Ed was shocked we found something so quickly and confessed he didn't think we would find something during the five days I was there.

"Faith, Uncle, gotta have faith." I spent the rest of my time in Mississippi taking Mom shopping for clothes, furniture, appliances … everything she needed to have a functional household. Dad had always been horribly cheap—Aunt Pat called him "miserly." I wanted Mom to have nice things, so I bought the best of everything. Between the deposit on the rental and new housewares, we spent ten thousand dollars in just a couple of days. I told Mom we needed to stop; she had the basics and she could get the rest later.

I spent my last two days with the Perry family, a brand-new experience. It delighted me to see Uncle Ron, Uncle Ed, and Mom all together—two brothers and their estranged sister, who had turned up after thirty-eight years and disrupted their lives. They had a chance for a new beginning. It wasn't that they were starting over, because I don't think there ever had been much of a start. Now they got to write their story in the later part of their lives and really enjoy each other.

The final and last drama of my sordid estate situation happened when I got home. The eviction process with the tenant in arrears had taken a turn for the worse. The renters had shown up in court dressed to the hilt in gold, satin, essentially their Sunday best, and tried to say they didn't owe any money or didn't have any, I can't remember. The court, of course, called it bullshit and issued a judgement against them on my behalf.

A few days later there was a "domestic dispute" at the house and the police got involved. The email I got from my attorney stated this:

"The family's attorney told me, however, that no one should go to the home as 'there is a potential police situation' happening at the house. Obviously, with this knowledge, I cannot send anyone over there."

I asked my attorney whether she expected to get the keys from them and she told me, "our office will not be accepting any keys" or anything else from them. I got the impression that they were afraid to have the renters at their office.

I knew that the man of the family was bat shit crazy. I could never get a straight answer out of him regarding rent, and he never made any sense, he talked in a strange drawl and in riddles. At the end of this ten-month journey, nothing surprised me anymore. If something could go wrong it did, and if it was strange and unprecedented, it happened. I had been putting out fires daily. When I read my attorney's email, I laughed. It was almost over anyway. The great unraveling of the biggest knots in the ancestral web was nearly finished. This was the last issue in the estate to be settled. Mom was good, all the houses were eventually sold, and I was a free bird.

CHAPTER 30

REFLECTIONS

Summer of 2016

Over the next few weeks, I sat with immense gratitude and marveled at how perfectly everything had worked out. If I had committed Mom in Michigan, she would have been alone and isolated, with no support once released. Someone would have to be responsible for her and her medication. I was relieved that, contingent upon her release from the hospital in Mississippi, there needed to be a person on record who would check on her, make sure she got to her clinic appointments, and took her medication. However reluctantly, her brothers stepped in and took on that responsibility.

When Dad died I had entered a transition state. An in-between place where a major loss has occurred, and I found myself temporarily poised between an old reality that has passed away and a new reality that has not yet fully formed. Going back to living my life as it had been before Dad died, was strange and felt completely out of alignment. Nothing fit, everything was too small. Yet I felt internally powerful. An inner strength had quietly birthed during this time, I knew at the core of my being, there wasn't anything I couldn't do. My connection with God grew. I had matured. There was no neediness. I didn't care what people thought of me. I found my voice. I let go of toxic relationships. I no longer had any desire to hide, and I started to slowly come into the world with my vulnerability.

To my dismay, I saw how all of my suffering over the previous ten months was part ancestral patterning and part self-inflicted behavior born out of childhood imprinting. My fear activated the inner controller/critic/judge, and I was not able to intelligently be with what was happening. I judged, I blamed, I condemned. Now that the ancestral pattering piece seemed to be unwinding and continually dissolving without much effort, my inner work was to begin to heal my childhood trauma. It became clear that I was living in a traumatized state, masked by being a *somewhat* highly functioning individual. I danced around it for years, indulging in retreats, meditation and other aversion-type gymnastics.

For the first time in my life, Mom and I are developing a relationship. I sent her Dad's cell phone, and we began texting each other every day. She never had a phone of her own and would always balk at me when I would text friends.

"Why do you want to text every five minutes. Don't you guys talk?" Once she started texting, she said, "Oh wow, this is fun. No wonder everyone loves to text." She's shared her great remorse that she didn't get on medication sooner. That she and Dad could have had a very different relationship and life. She still triggers me but at least I can talk to her about things and she's generally present and listening. All I ever really wanted was to feel that she cared.

In the months after her release from the hospital, Mom got dentures, had cataract surgery in both eyes, lost fifty pounds, walked or ran more than eight 10K marathons with her best friend, Carole, (she has a wall full of ribbons to prove it), reconnected with friends and family, and frequently went to Memphis to see shows and musicals with her high school friends. For all practical purposes, she is a normal functioning human being. She struggles with her memory, and I get horribly impatient, but statistically speaking, Mom is a miracle. The fact that she has stayed on her meds and is doing really well is rare with such cases. This keeps me in perpetual gratitude.

I am convinced that the transformation that is currently my mother occurred because of the power of prayer, the ancestor liberation homas done at Oneness University, and the fact that I followed through with what I see as my soul contract of helping my mom. It becomes ever clearer to me, even though it's easy to forget, that, without God, I can do nothing that is important, I cannot grow, I cannot love, I cannot fulfill what I was put on this earth to do, I can do nothing without the Creator. I traveled more than 14,000 miles in ten months held in a benevolent embrace.

CHAPTER 31

MY DEEPEST WISH

It was surprising to learn that both my attorney and realtor had experiences that were nearly identical to mine at the same time as I did, i.e., someone died and all their affairs defaulted to someone who was mentally ill. During this process, I continued to meet people who knew someone with schizophrenia, and they talked about the incredible difficulty it creates for the families as well as the mentally ill person. It's a tragedy as everyone involved feels alone, isolated, and frustrated by the lack of resources for help.

It's my deepest prayer and wish that the laws are changed around mental illness. That it's not so hard for individuals to be committed and get effective treatment. As it stands right now, to petition a family member into a hospital they have to be a danger to themselves or others. Why do we have to wait for something bad to happen? It's a scientific fact that the disease of schizophrenia, over time, gets worse not better. Can early intervention prevent the disease from progressing? For the most part our current medical model is "we'll take action during a crisis," the proverbial wait-and-see, which makes no sense to me. What about simple neglect, as was demonstrated on my first trip home when my unbathed mom was wearing holey clothes, had no teeth, and was partially blind? I would say this represents a harm and danger to the self. Personal neglect has horrible consequences, taking a toll on what little self-worth and self-esteem is present. Mentally ill people should not be treated like criminals and sent to jail without food or water for days while waiting for a hospital bed to become available.

Mom was lucky that she had her brothers to go to upon her release, but I know there are a lot of individuals who don't have a loving family around them, so they end up on the street again. This is unacceptable. They need loving attention, care, a safe shelter and deep restful sleep. High quality healthy nutrition free from processed food and sugar is non-negotiable. Again, there is a plethora of information available on nutrition and mental health. There need to be better types of medication that don't produce a lot of side effects. And, lastly, second in importance to nutrition, is a sense of purpose. Every individual on the planet needs to feel like they have a purpose or are good at something … otherwise depression commonly takes hold. Even though Mom didn't leave the house much she had many activities in the house that brought her a lot of joy. She did woodworking, built furniture, became what I consider a master gardener. These things brought meaning to her life. We, as a society, have a tremendous amount of work to do in helping and treating people with brain disease labeled as mental illness.

CHAPTER 32

FOUR YEARS LATER

Summer 2020

As the years have gone by, there has been a tremendous ease and flow in life for both my mom and me. I don't want to blame Dad, but it was as if Mom and I could not move forward personally while Dad was here. We were stuck in very self-destructive versions of ourselves that, no matter what we did, we could not escape from. I asked Mom what life is like for her now and she says she has good days and bad days. Sometimes she doesn't feel mentally and emotionally stable. She gets anxiety frequently. "I wonder if I can handle this day if the car breaks down? Did I remember to pay my bills? I have to double check that I paid all my bills—I have to write it down. It gets quiet and lonely at home by myself. And what if I fall or get sick? I wish I had another single friend—everyone is married with families and husbands."

I asked her if she still has memory loss and if she enjoys being as social as she is now.

"I don't feel like I have the bad memory loss anymore," she said. "Thankfully I don't have the paranoia of being followed anymore, I guess that's the risperidone medication." Mom was initially on Geodon but was quickly switched to Risperidone due to Geodon's side effects. Mom has a very active social life, more than me actually! She is always hanging out with her childhood friends, and she now works at Sigma Pi frat house at the University of Mississippi—we just call it *Ole Miss.* "I really enjoy it because I keep my days busy. Connecting with others, I don't like being alone all the time at home. You go crazy being by yourself all the time. But sometimes after working all week, I need downtime."

Sadly, Uncle Ed died of a heart attack on January 15th, 2019. Mom says, "Reconnecting with family has been so wonderful and I'm happy that Ed and I had those years together. Even though he said I got on his nerves all the time." Mom laughs, "family is so important, nice to have such a good time. I miss going to his house and talking to him. He knew something about everything, I always learned something."

I asked her what it's like having a relationship with me now. "I really enjoy talking and sharing with you about what's going on in our lives. We aren't fighting constantly like we used to. We feel like sisters." It's funny she said this because I feel like we're sisters, too. I asked if she would want to get remarried. "No marriage, but I'd like to hang out. I would love to just have a companion." I've seen a huge evolution in my mother since she moved to Oxford. As long as she is on her meds—which, thankfully, is most of the time—she takes responsibility for her own life, taking care of herself and filling her time with enjoyable and productive activities. She has softened and has become more loving and kind and supportive. I've been able to talk to her about what's going on in my life without worrying that she is going to condemn me for every little detail.

Meanwhile, I've evolved, too. Mom recognizes now how hard it must have been for me to grow up with her being the way she was, and there has been tremendous healing in that validation. I've come to value mental health as a huge resource for us in life and know it's something we must never take for granted. We each have our own struggles, but we also never know what challenges other people are facing.

In the years that followed Dad's death, layers of my personality, beliefs, and ideals have continued to get stripped away and changed. That in-between space I talked about earlier continued, and it's been a very slow process, one of expansion and contraction in consciousness. I finally stopped smoking on October 20th, 2017, after twenty-two years. It took four months of weekly hypnosis sessions. Once the nicotine addiction fell away, along with its purpose of keeping me relatively numb, I was really met with how much I didn't like being a business owner and felt I was professionally at a dead end with it. I realized I loved studying the medicine but didn't enjoy the practice. For more than a decade, I had thought about finishing my biology degree. I really missed doing laboratory work and feel that this was truly my first love as a career choice. So, in the fall of 2018, I enrolled at Sonoma State University and miraculously was able to get credit for my previous education. My final degree was a BS in Cellular and Molecular Biology with a minor in Chemistry. Going back to school at age forty-three was difficult, but no harder than anything else I've done. I had to overcome the belief that I wasn't smart enough, which was part of the reason I had dropped out of school back in 1995. I graduated in May of 2021 and am aiming to become a clinical lab scientist.

Chris and I amicably parted ways, and I am forever grateful for his support at a time I was so overwhelmed and confused. He gave me a place to land both emotionally and physically.

I'm still working on unraveling trauma and hurt. It will likely be a lifelong process. But at this point I've let go of the idea that anything outside of myself will save me: a guru, a teaching, a formal spiritual path. The things that help the most are meeting myself wherever I am every day with love and compassion. I've adopted an embodiment practice that has helped me integrate my pain more than meditations and teachings ever did. My intention is simply to be as honest as I can with myself by listening within and following that guidance. My goal is to master my internal sensations and emotions and to have autonomy and sovereignty over my being and my life. I have a very small tight inner circle of friends, but they are priceless in their love and acceptance of me. I continue to deepen my relationship with God. All of this has led me to the very beginning of a new and fulfilling life.

TRANSCRIPT OF INTERVIEW WITH SUSAN MOORE

The Following is an interview with Mom conducted by my editor, Laurel Kashinn.

Laurel Kashinn: **First, I just want to extend my condolences. I am so sorry for the loss of your husband.**

Susan Moore: Thank you. I appreciate that.

Laurel: **What has it been it like for you, the journey you have been on these past few years?**

Susan: I went from having a nice home, living in Michigan, to suddenly having nothing. I lost my husband, I lost my house, I went from living a nice middle-class life to being all alone.

It's a big challenge. I never worked outside the home in my entire life. I never supported myself or made an income. Now, all of a sudden I'm having to do everything. I feel like I'm sixty-seven going on eighteen. When I lived in Michigan, my husband did everything. Now I'm having to pay the bills, and deal with my illness. I just hope things don't get bad again.

Laurel: **Tell me about your family growing up. What was your life like before you got married?**

Susan: I had three brothers and grew up in the South. I always thought I got this mental illness from my dad. He was very antisocial. He didn't have friends, he didn't socialize, and he didn't want to socialize. I also had some mentally challenged cousins.

Laurel: So, there was something in the family.

Susan: Yes. Neither of my parents were real sociable. They were very hard workers and all, and they definitely provided for us, but there was a lack of emotional support and presence. They were not very educated people. They did the best they could. We always had a roof over our heads and food to eat. But, as far as socialization, it was pretty lacking.

As for the mental illness, I was the one who got it all. My brothers are okay, and they are all very accomplished. One is a doctor, one an attorney and one was a teacher. Me, I was never good at anything. I never had an interest in anything. I drifted. I never was ambitious, never knew what I wanted. And I had a learning disability and had a hard time in school. Hated it. Didn't do well in school. I didn't want to be there.

Then I met my husband and got married and started staying home. Staying home, that was when I discovered talents I didn't know I had. I did woodworking, I sewed, and I did gardening and landscaping. I was a late bloomer. I discovered my talents in my forties.

Laurel: **How did you and your husband meet?**

Susan: I was living in California with my mother after her divorce. He was sent there for work at Ford Motor Company. Ford had test labs all over the country. He was sent out to do some testing. Some of my cousins worked with him. They set us up on a blind date.

Laurel: **Do you remember what you felt when you met him?**

Susan: I thought he was nice and personable. I liked him. He was in California and we dated that whole time. He left California and went back to Michigan. We stayed in touch. He flew back out at Christmas and asked me to come back to Michigan. At first, I said, 'I don't know.' But then I said 'yes.'

Heather Moore: **You just married him that fast?**

Susan: He was in California for ten months, we dated all those ten months, and when he left, we stayed in touch.

Laurel:	**So, you got married, where?**
Susan:	We got married in Michigan.
Laurel:	**Moving to Michigan, what was that like?**
Susan:	It was fine. I liked it. I found I liked it a lot. I've always been a cold weather person. I love the cold and the snow. I really don't like the heat and humidity. I really enjoyed Michigan, thoroughly.
Laurel:	**So, you moved to Michigan. What happened then?**
Susan:	A year later, after we were married, Heather was born. She was our only child.
Laurel:	**You had a child, and your husband worked. Did you feel isolated?**
Susan:	Yes, but that didn't bother me. I enjoyed being alone. I was never a social butterfly. All the activities at home kept me busy. As long as I was doing something, making things or involved in things at home, I was happy. I just didn't socialize.
	It is still challenging now. I moved back here and it's like starting all over again. I have a hard time finding things to keep me busy. In Michigan I had the house and the garden to keep me busy. And the woodworking. Now I rent.

Laurel:	**Tell me about your experience getting arrested.**
Susan:	It was awful. My brother had me committed. In Mississippi, they put you in jail while you wait for a bed. I was in jail for three or four days. I was completely isolated. It was a very humbling experience. There was nothing. No TV, no radio.
	I was in jail and then I was transported to North Mississippi State Hospital, where I stayed for one month. I was diagnosed with schizophrenia. They put me on medication. The medication seems to be working pretty well.
Laurel:	**How have things changed for you?**
Susan:	I always felt someone was following me. That feeling is gone now. The medicine seems to be working.
Laurel:	**How about the cost of the medication? Is it very expensive?**
Susan:	No. The medication is not expensive. $10 per month.
	I'm just thankful that I'm mobile, that I can get up and walk around. I get up and thank God I can get up and get dressed and walk around and cook for myself. I thank God.
Laurel:	**I hear you're now doing marathons.**

Susan:	Yes. I always have enjoyed walking, and I have a friend who runs marathons. When I came back to Mississippi, we hooked up again. Since I got here, I've done some 5K runs and will do a 10K in December. Now I walk eight miles a day. Walking really helps you sleep well, too, that's why I like it. You get a good night's sleep.
Laurel:	**During those years you were ill, before the meds, how important were your wood-working and gardening hobbies?**
Susan:	I don't know what would have happened if I didn't have the activities I had. If I was busy, I was so happy. If I didn't have that, I don't know what would have happened. You've got to have something to get your mind off your problems. I was very lucky my husband allowed me to do all those things. The more isolated I was, the more creative I became.
Heather:	The nice thing is Dad went out and bought you tools and plants. Dad gave you the outlet.
Laurel:	**What if you could do woodworking again?**
Susan:	I would like that. But to do woodworking would be difficult. There's no place to do it. I'm in Oxford, Mississippi. It's a college town, and it's very expensive to live here. There's no place for that.

Heather: Could you do it in your apartment?

Susan: No, I wouldn't want it in the house, with all the sawdust. I would need a shop.

Laurel: **What happened to the woodworking pieces you made?**

Susan: We lost all of the pieces. Left them behind in Athens, Georgia. The only thing I have left from my life before was a bag of clothes and an umbrella.

Laurel: **Do you miss being able to do woodworking? What if you started a business woodworking?**

Susan: It would be nice to have a woodworking studio again. Having a business would be very expensive. That is out of sight. I don't see how that could happen.

Heather: Mom's friend, Diane, is a woodworker. Mom, maybe you could work at her place.

Susan: Maybe. Or work in a garden center part time.

Laurel: **How are things different for you now?**

Susan: My thought patterns are clearer on the medications. I used to be very impulsive. It was always very hard to concentrate. I was scatterbrained. That was always a big problem. Now, with the medication, it helps me to concentrate a lot better. I am clear and can think through the problems.

Heather:	My experience of Mom is she's a lot more present. Before I would share things with her, emotional things like, "I'm not feeling well." Or "I broke up with my boyfriend." And there was no response. Now she can console me. I feel concern in her voice. Before, we couldn't connect. It was like an empty space.
Susan:	Now I can concentrate and hear what you're saying.
	They say with the meds you have to take it the rest of your life. I also have some dementia, short-term memory loss. Can't remember things from ten or fifteen minutes ago. My mother died of Alzheimer's.
	Now I'm older, and it is scary. You think about deteriorating further.
Heather:	Mom doesn't really see how much the medication is helping. Now, for the first time in my life, she's actually my mom.
Susan:	I was drifting around in la-la land half the time.
	I just wish I had been on medication a lot sooner. I wish I had been diagnosed earlier, gotten on medication sooner, gotten treatment earlier. I think I've had this all my life and I'm sixty-seven now. If I'd known sooner, my life would have been far different. You can tell when things are off. I always knew but couldn't pinpoint it. Never felt normal.

The thing is, when you're ill you know you need help, but you don't know what you need. Being committed was the only way I could have gotten into a hospital. I can tell you, I would not have voluntarily done it. There needs to be a better way. People don't seek treatment or won't get it, because they don't think they need it. As it is now, being committed, that's the only way

Heather: At the time, for all those years, Mom, you never thought there was anything wrong with you. There was the Guardian ad litem in Michigan, who was appointed by the court to interview Mom to determine Mom's mental state. Went to court with attorney. Guardian ad litem can go to court and testify. All of it could be done in a much more humane way.

Laurel: **What is your advice for others who suffer from mental illness?**

Susan: Learn all you can about it. I don't think people really understand mental illness. It's never been acceptable. It's always been a taboo kind of thing. With mental illness, there are no rational thoughts. I have a niece who is bipolar. We don't think like you think. People say, "why did you do that?" When your thought patterns are all messed up it is depressing. No one understands.

Heather:	There are definitely cycles. Good for years.
Susan:	I'm thankful that we've had the opportunity to grow closer and have a mother-daughter relationship.
Heather:	Me too. It's a journey. And it's a journey you can't take by yourself.
Susan:	I love you, Heather.
Heather:	I love you, too, Mom.

*   *   *

SCHIZOPHRENIA RESOURCES

Below are the organizations and resources that helped me understand schizophrenia, specifically how to better show up for mom, how to take care of myself especially with setting boundaries, and generally how to feel safe and grounded while navigating mom's disease.

National Organizations:

Schizophrenia & Psychosis Action Alliance, website - https://sczaction.org

Their Caregiver toolkit is amazing, the best resource to start with.

National Alliance on Mental Illness (NAMI), website - https://www.nami.org.

Family to family class is wonderful community support.

Treatment Advocacy Center (TAC), website - https://www.tac.org

Helps you understand and find treatment the different treatment options across the country.

Successful treatment requires a 4-pronged approach: medication, diet, social support and therapy. In talking with others diet is wildly underutilized and probably the most helpful. Mom had a significant shift in her mood, sleep and energy when she switched to a keto based diet. Researchers and Psychiatrists,

Dr. James Greenblatt and Dr. Chris Palmer, are trailblazing the nutritional psychiatry pathway. I've included some podcasts below to get you started.

The Mental Health Crisis No One's Talking About with Dr. James Greenblatt

https://www.youtube.com/watch?v=lpiUpNYchsQ

Functional Medicine Psychiatry – Getting to the Root Cause of Mental Illness

https://drhyman.com/blogs/content/podcast-ep902/

Is the Ketogenic Diet Effective in Treating Schizophrenia?

https://www.youtube.com/watch?v=ej8MvCdg4NE

Family and Caregiver Manuals/Books:

Surviving Schizophrenia (E. Fuller Torrey, MD): A highly-regarded family manual that covers causes, symptoms, treatments, and practical advice for families and patients.

The Complete Family Guide to Schizophrenia (Kim T. Meuser & Susan Gingerich): Offers practical strategies for managing crises, improving communication, and encouraging recovery for your loved one.

I Am Not Sick, I Don't Need Help! (Xavier Amador, Ph.D.): A crucial guide that teaches the LEAP method to help a loved one with anosognosia (lack of insight into their illness) accept treatment

The Body Keeps the Score (Bessel van der Kolk, MD): Explains complex trauma and how to heal from it. This booked helped me see I wasn't crazy and explained that most of my dysregulation was from having a mother with mental illness. After I read this book I felt like I could finally heal.

A book for the children who have a parent with mental illness.

ACKNOWLEDGMENTS

My unwavering and immense gratitude goes to the following people for without their emotional and physical support, my story would look very different and this book would not have been written.

My mom, Susan Moore for her willingness to work on herself and grow. Her devotion to our relationship and her sincere effort to help repair the wreckage of my childhood. Her generous financial support for the editing and publishing of this book and my life in general.

My family, Aunt Pat for your financial support in the first months of Dad's death and emotional support since then. You're the best Auntie ever! Aunt Pat, Uncle Steve, cousin Kelly and Danny for helping pack the moving truck and for the herculean task of cleaning out the garage and basement. Uncle Ron and to my late Uncle Ed for stepping in despite your resistance. Mom and I are grateful for the reunion.

To Paul Burns for giving me the idea and pushing me to write this book.

To Chris Collins for providing peace and a place to land in the midst of all the mayhem and madness. Your patience and support in my many false starts gave me time to figure out next steps. You are incredibly generous.

To my healers Lokpal and Walker Whelan, for being available at nearly any hour, supporting me emotionally and energetically. Clearing my space, providing guidance, and helping illuminate the path with mom.

To the one I call "my guardian angel" Soreliz Ascanio, your friendship is the bar for all other friendships. You have the most amazing heart I have ever known. Generous in your wisdom, never judgmental, all loving and accepting.

To my soul siStars in Salt Lake City: Sara Supinski, Annie Asher and Carly Chouinard. Your individual ability to see me, energetically hold me and love me, mirrored myself back to me. Your devotion to our friendship and your reflection allowed me for the first time in my life, to clearly see and believe in my value on a soul level. This is the greatest gift anyone could ever give. A deep bow to my besties.

To Curt Ruegsegger my partner in life and growth. You are the greatest mirror, revealing my shadow and exposing my deepest unhealed parts. Demanding me to be present and slow down, brought an elevated dimension of clarity and meaning to the extensive editing process of the manuscript. The book grew as I grew. Sincere admiration for the space, patience and encouragement you have provided as we both evolve in this crazy life.

To my first editor Laurel Kashinn for never letting me give up on this project. I wrote the first draft of my manuscript in the summer of 2016 and started working with Laurel shortly thereafter. As the years went by there was delay after delay in funding and feedback. I started wavering on whether I wanted to scrap the manuscript. But Laurel kept the idea alive with nudging emails or a text once in a while so the flame wouldn't go out. Thank you Laurel for believing in my vision and not letting me give up.

To my second editor Susan Crossman who listened to me for hours and really brought the manuscript to a whole other level with clarity and impact and for introducing me to my amazing team:

My publisher Susie Schaefer, for her Oracle card readings in the beginning that set the tone for the whole project: Master teacher, soul destiny and a shit load of invisible help. The only outcome is success. Julia Kurtis for the perfect book cover. Julie Balgavy for the most gorgeous photos.

And finally to all the generous donors of my 2018 GoFundMe campaign. Deep appreciation to the family and friends who donated and for your belief and support in my vision.

Superheroes
Susan Moore

Jeffery Packer

Olivia Dacre-Lawson

Emily Anderson

Liselot Bergen

Neil McKechnie

Janis Eggleston

Martha Perry

Melissa Dooley

Georgia Wright

Kelli Fiore and Brenda Scaman

Soreliz Ascanio

Elizabeth Scherwenka

Laurie Hebert

Sandy Quinones

Jonathan Armen

Anonymous #1

Heroes

Patricia Lutke

Michelle Olsen

Julie Stevenson

Kayla Bilger

Liberators

Graham Quigley

Patti Covell

Beth Clarke

Anonymous #2

Anonymous #3

ABOUT THE AUTHOR

Heather Moore has dedicated decades of her life to restoring the physical and emotional landscapes of wellness, having practiced as both a licensed acupuncturist and a functional medicine practitioner—among numerous other qualifications. She has degrees in molecular biology and Chinese Medicine and she is a tireless advocate for helping people enhance their vitality.

Having lived much of her life in communities with a coast, Heather's life underscores the metaphorical nexus between the fluidity of the energetic world and the physical reality of the land on which we stand.

Her compelling first book, *Trusting Resilience*, shares the story of her harrowing relationship with her schizophrenic mother and the heart-wrenching commitment they both made, despite the odds, to letting love win.

www.ingramcontent.com/pod-product-compliance
Lightning Source LLC
Chambersburg PA
CBHW051249250726
48656CB00004B/1195